The New Industrial
Organization

The New Industrial Organization

Market Forces and Strategic Behavior

Alexis Jacquemin

Translated by
Fatemeh Mehta

The MIT Press
Cambridge, Massachusetts
London, England

© 1987 Massachusetts Institute of Technology

This work was originally published in French under the title *Sélection et pouvoir dans la nouvelle économie industrielle,* © 1985 by Cabay Libraire-Editeur, Louvain-la-Neuve, Belgium.

This book was set in Palatino by Achorn Graphic Services and printed and bound by Halliday Lithograph in the United States of America.

Library of Congress Cataloging-in-Publication Data

Jacquemin, Alex.
   The new industrial organization.

   Translation of: Sélection et pouvoir dans la nouvelle
économie industrielle.
   Includes bibliographies and index.
   1. Industrial organization (Economic theory)
2. Oligopolies.   3. Barriers to entry (Industrial
organization)   I. Title.
HD2326.J313   1987   338.6   86-20039
ISBN 0-262-10035-5
ISBN 0-262-60014-5   (pbk.)

To Brigitte

Contents

Preface

This work is the fruit of an initiative on the part of the University of Liège, which invited me to occupy the Francqui Chair and give a series of lectures during the 1984–1985 academic year.

The theme of the work has been inspired by a certain radicalization of positions vis-à-vis our decentralized economies, a radicalization that has no doubt been encouraged by the crisis. In the light of recent works in industrial organization, it seemed useful to present the analyses that underlie such positions and to show their contributions and also their limits and the dangers inherent in their normative use.

Although this work is principally based on theoretical studies and uses empirical research only occasionally, technical analyses in the text have been deliberately limited, and the notes provide suggestions for further development of the ideas and for complementary reading. For this reason each chapter incorporates corresponding notes and references.

Before delivering myself to the invisible reader or being relegated to the "hypothetical shelf," as Italo Calvino calls it, I must thank C. d'Aspremont, P. Dehez, and P. Regibeau, who, by agreeing to read one version of this text, have perhaps enabled me to reach a second best solution.

My acknowledgment is equally addressed to my colleague D. Encaoua for his constant intellectual support. I am also grateful to E. Chiostri, whose patience and typing competence overcame a stubborn manuscript, and to Fatemeh Mehta, for her careful translation.

As regards the European University Institute in Florence, where I completed the manuscript, it has been an ideal place of reception where fruitful scientific exchanges could be reconciled with a (quasi-)monastic peace.

The New Industrial
Organization

1   Approaches to Industrial Organization

The purpose of this chapter is twofold: to contrast the theoretical and empirical approaches traditionally adopted in industrial organization with those developed in recent years and to use this new context to put into perspective the recurring debate between the proponents of "natural" adaptation of industry to environmental conditions and those whose analysis focuses on the "strategic" dimension and the manipulation of environment.

1.1 Classical Industrial Organization

To analyze a market, either from the viewpoint of a firm operating (or envisaging entry) in the market or that of public authorities trying to evaluate the existing situation in order to formulate the rules of the game, it is necessary to describe the market. Hitherto the principal aim of most research in industrial organization has been precisely to provide this description by referring to the usual classical paradigm relating market structures, the behavior of economic agents, and their resulting performance. The basic questions, whether they concern a company or a public authority responsible for antitrust or industrial policy, remain similar. So far as market structures are concerned, the questions relate to the number of competitors in the market and to the distribution of the market shares in the activity, to the degree of strictness of the conditions of entry and exit, to the standardization of the product and its relative proximity to substitutes, to the existing vertical integration of the activity, to the quantity of information retained by participants, and to the importance of the risks encountered. With regard to economic behavior, the questions must determine the respective roles of price and non-price strategies, the level of cooperation attained among agents over time, the application of strategies of differentiation and diversification, and so on. Finally, the examination of outcomes, whether in terms of resource allocation, observed profitability, or growth, would complete the approach.

Such a study of structure, behavior, and performance should then make it possible to answer a fundamental question: What form does competition take in the market? Naturally, the sense of the question varies according to who poses it. For public authorities the intention is to determine whether or not the natural forces of competition inherent in the market lead to an efficient allocation of resources and to socially acceptable distributions. From the enterprise's point of view, it is important to know whether its current or prospective relative position is sufficiently differentiated, protected, and "imperfect" for it to extract a substantial profit.

Several studies in the literature on industrial organization have provided a useful framework, and they allow the identification and classification of some complex competitive phenomena of industrial society. They have bequeathed a certain substance to the famous "empty boxes" of traditional microeconomic analysis. Nevertheless, until the 1960s a great many authors had employed a dangerously restrictive perspective.

It is worth emphasizing two shortcomings of the classical industrial organization, one theoretical and the other empirical. On the theoretical level the effort to place the analysis within the context of a well-defined microeconomic model has often been lacking, and the precise form of oligopolistic interdependence has rarely been explicitly defined. On the contrary, emphasis has been placed on describing market structures and their direct links with realized performance. The role of agents' behavior is minimized in the sense that firms are assumed to have the same objective and to adapt themselves more or less passively to their industrial environment.

Let S, C, and P be variables representing sets of market structure, conduct, and performance, respectively. "Structuralist" authors would write

$$C = C(S),$$
$$P = P(C, S) = \phi(S).$$

From this viewpoint industrial organization is a model in which change is treated as exogenous and where behavior and performance are structurally determined. It is also a static sytem (or rather a comparative static one) that does not take into account that competition is an evolving and historic process with possibilities of interactions, going, for instance, from performance to behavior and from behavior to certain structures that thus become endogenous.

On the empirical level two types of study characterize the traditional outlook: case studies and econometric studies. Case studies, which were particularly prolific in the 1960s, have provided a better understanding of some industries and of some markets. The consideration of qualitative aspects has clarified the complexity of industrial reality, whereas quantitative measures, such as the degree of concentration or the profit rate, have provided simple summary indicators of the observed situation. These many cases, however, have not given rise to much hope that a general outline can be made and further developed.

After the 1960s econometric studies increased and set themselves the task of going beyond the limit of case studies by finding statistically significant links between some indicators of performance, such as the profit rate, and a whole set of indicators of market structure, in particular, the degree of concentration. These regressions have been based on cross sections of industries. Their objective is essentially to test simple hypotheses, possibly applicable to all markets, such as the existence of a linear relationship between the degree of concentration and the rate of profitability in the industry. The theoretical arguments that are used to include or exclude a particular structural aspect from a list of explanatory variables are often ad hoc, made without any clear reference to an underlying general model of which the tested equation is the reduced form. Moreover, the interpretation is a causal one—ceteris paribus, a high degree of concentration should result in a higher rate of profit—rather than an equilibrium relationship.

The obvious weaknesses of this approach should not, however, make us forget that it is often under the pressure of the questions raised in the applied literature on industrial organization that theorists have gradually been led to abandon the reassuring foundations of traditional models and to provide a rigorous basis for concepts and perspectives hitherto undiscovered. Moreover, we should remember that many of those who have studied industrial organization have already noted these shortcomings and have enriched the microeconomic theory of their time by incorporating new behavioral hypotheses. As we will see, this is particularly the case for the theory of "limit pricing" and the organizational theory of the firm.

Recently, traditional approaches have been renewed, leading to what some do not hesitate to call "the new industrial organization" (Schmalensee 1982). I describe this next.

1.2 Features of the New Industrial Organization

What has come to be known as the new industrial organization presents innovative methodological aspects, and, moreover, it relaunches on the basis of more technical analysis the eternal debate between those who see in our industrial economies an efficient adaptation to external technological conditions and those who see complex games of power and economic domination in them.

Methodological Aspects

Compared with earlier studies, recent research increasingly is using tools of microeconomic theory, models of imperfect competition, and notions of game theory. Going beyond the extreme cases of perfect competition and monopoly, concepts of solution grow in number, such as Stackelberg's price leadership, Cournot-Nash equilibrium, and monopolistic competition. Oligopolistic interdependence has been explained as much in terms of cooperative games as by models of noncooperative behavior.

Furthermore, dynamics in industrial structure has come to replace static approaches. Schumpeter (1950) has already stressed the intertemporal framework within which the competitive process should be placed.

The best way to realistically visualise industrial strategies is to observe the conduct of new organisations . . . who introduce new products or new processes . . . or who reorganise a part or whole of an industry. (p. 83)

We must therefore assume that economic agents are making sequential decisions and taking into account the consequences of their actions on the subsequent evolution of industrial activity. This approach leads to the use not only of dynamic programming methods, optimal control theory, and differential games but also to the economic history of industries and firms. It also allows for the fact that within this context buyers and sellers do not have perfect knowledge of the particulars of their partners or adversaries, their preferences, or their means. Situations of complete and incomplete information are treated differently, and new concepts of equilibrium are developed (perfect equilibrium, Bayesian equilibrium).

These methodological perspectives have an important implication. Rather than looking for *the* model which permits simple generalizations that can be applied to most industries, as previous authors would have liked, it seems inevitable that we must develop a whole range of models from which one model specific to the market under study can be selected. Contrary to monism, such eclecticism is paradoxically similar to the concern of losing, as a result of modeling, the qualitative richness of the information supplied by case studies. Monism and eclecticism may in fact be complementary, in the sense that the model can be adapted to the major observed features of the industry, namely its structure, its behavioral patterns, and its performance. Beyond this a typology of behavior and markets can be made to correspond to appropriate models.

Empirically, the econometric analysis based on inter-industry cross sections that is plagued by many problems of interpretation has been complemented by time series analyses of the same industry on the one hand and by intra-industrial comparisons on the other, where the heterogeneity of economic agents, their performance, and their strategies within the same industry can be tested.

The Renewal of an Endemic Debate

The setting up of models and hypotheses follows not only the path of logic but also a whole set of presuppositions tied to the social and political context in which they are developed. In one way or another we can always maintain that scientific thought is deeply rooted in social reality. Ladriere (1976) writes:

Such a context can only be elucidated by taking into account the implicit (and perhaps explicit) projects upon which it is based. (p. 7)

It is, for example, clearly admitted in economics that determining the requisite conditions for the coherence of a decentralized system, whose efficiency is ensured by prices, is totally different from demonstrating its conformity with existing markets. Nevertheless the development of models rapidly leads to judgments on their relevance to the real economy and to assertions of political economy that may well go beyond the narrow limits of the adopted theoretical framework.

The issue is particularly delicate in evaluating the role of the search for technical efficiency and the role of market power in observed economic behavior. This debate, which has always underlain industrial economics, reappears in most works on the "new industrial organization" in a more rigorous form. Two viewpoints can be distinguished in the literature. The first one considers that productive structures, existing market forms, and organizational methods adopted by enterprises are a good approximation of the efficient adaptation that should result from some external order dictated by the existing technology.

Given the output vector in a specific market as well as the monetary value of the required physical *and* organizational inputs, the natural market structure will emerge, that is, the one in which the corresponding monetary value of inputs is lower than the monetary value of inputs required for any other possible allocation of outputs. Minimization of both production and transaction costs is then obtained.

In contrast, the second viewpoint stresses the role of economic agents modifying their environment instead of being subjected to predetermined conditions. These are innovators of combinations and of new forms; they can manipulate their environment and can determine to some extent market conditions. In this perspective the configuration of industrial structures and organizational forms is as much the outcome of deliberate strategies as of initial conditions and predetermined rules of the game. Referring back to the functional relationship between market structure and realized performance, one can, for instance, consider the evolution over time of market structure to be determined by a transformation that depends not only on structure at moment t and on time but also on conducts C.

These two approaches, which incidentally are not necessarily totally contradictory, must be put in a wider intellectual framework in which ideological presuppositions are increasingly evident. In fact, one can envisage the evolution of our industrial societies as a selection process in which the fittest economic agents, social groups, nations, and institutions emerge. Hierarchies and the dominance of certain forms would then be the outcome of a selective filtering process and of a diffused competition tending to maximum efficiency.

Economic and social institutions, the distribution of income, and the international division of labor are expressions of the adaptation to a "natural" order dictated by technology, factor endowments, and qualifications and productivity of individuals. These notions are similar to some ideas of classical economics, such as those of Adam

Smith, and today find a new dimension in the application of sociobiology to economics. In contrast, other analyses portray the economic agent, be it the firm or the state, as striving to orient its evolution, to use innovation in order to provoke ruptures, to impose new norms and new forms of equilibrium, rather than to submit to the environment: Some economic agents alter the institutions and the rules of the game; the comparative advantages between nations are partly fabricated or imposed; income inequalities are partly the outcome of actions of groups defending their interests and more fundamentally depend on the underlying sociocultural relations. The main driving force behind the undeniable process of evolution is therefore not a mechanical selection, and its logic is not merely the requirements of the environment.

It is well known that "competition between paradigms is not the kind of battle that can be won with proofs" (Kuhn 1970, p. 204). Rather than trying to resolve a debate, the purpose of this book, as explained in the next section, is to throw some light on the two approaches presented in the preceding paragraphs. My preferences will nevertheless not remain undisclosed!

1.3 The Subject Matter of This Book

The rest of this book is a series of essays aimed at presenting in a simple form some of the analyses of the new industrial organization applied to the enterprise, its market relations, and its internal organization.

In order to outline the major features of these works and their possible implications for economic policy, the following presentation is adopted: contrasting the perspective that industrial economy adapts itself to the norms of an efficient allocation of resources with that which stresses the role of market power.

The second chapter is devoted to selective market mechanisms. The hypothesis of profit maximization, dynamic competition, and long-term stationary equilibrium of an industry are analyzed in the context of the Darwinian outlook of adaptation to environmental constraints.

In the third chapter I discuss the behavior of corporations trying to exploit oligopolistic interdependencies. A discussion of the significance of the degree of concentration is followed by the presentation and comparison of various models of oligopoly in price and quantity.

The role of potential competition is introduced in chapter 4. The analysis of its favorable effects as a market discipline is followed by a comparison of "natural" and "strategic" barriers. Static and dynamic models of entry are then presented, shedding some light on conditions of market power.

I discuss the organizational forms adopted by the enterprise in chapter 5. I begin by describing theories according to which the choice of the organizational form is designed to minimize transaction costs within the firm. The multiplicity and coexistence of different forms of organization are then studied, raising the question of the predominant form. The organizational form is finally considered as a strategic variable that might help the firm exercise control over the market.

The sixth chapter is devoted to the different roles assigned to industrial policy, depending on whether the emphasis is placed on spontaneous adjustment to market forces or on strategic behavior. It leads ultimately to the choice of the model of *society*. Beyond Darwinian analogies, sociobiology and bioeconomics propose a model of society based on natural selection, that is, a set of mechanisms sorting out individuals, organizations, and institutions that are most suited. In contrast, there is a model of society in which evolution preserves diversity and in which the behavior of agents can mold environment to a great extent toward their objectives and can control it by deliberate choices.

References

T. Kuhn. 1970. *The Structure of Scientific Revolutions,* second edition. Chicago: University of Chicago Press.

J. Ladriere. 1976. Preface to *La philosophie de K. Popper et le positivisme logique* (The philosophy of K. Popper and logical positivism), by J. F. Malherbe. Paris: PUF.

R. Schmalensee. 1982. "The new industrial organization and the economic analysis of modern markets," in *Advances in Economic Theory,* W. Hildenbrand (ed.). Cambridge: Cambridge University Press, 253–285.

J. Schumpeter. 1950. *Capitalism, Socialism, and Democracy.* London: Allen and Unwin.

2 Selective Market Processes

The use of biological analogies in economics is an old tradition. Many authors, among them Adam Smith, Alfred Marshall and, more recently, Kenneth Boulding, Armen Alchian, Hendrik Houthakker, Gary Becker, and Jack Hirshleifer, have employed this approach and used such concepts as natural selection, life cycle, and homeostasis to describe certain economic phenomena. More systematically, it has recently been argued that the fundamental concepts that make up the dominant analytical structure of economics and biology are strictly analogous: Notions such as scarcity, competition, equilibrium, and specialization play similar roles in both domains. The notion of species could correspond to industry, mutation to innovation, evolution to progress, genetic heredity to imitation, and "mutualism" to exchange. Moreover, some strongly believe that economics, like the whole of social sciences devoted to the study of mankind, is but a subdivision of sociobiology. Sociobiology, according to Edward Wilson (1975), is concerned with the interrelations among various forms of life—organisms, species, and groups in the wider sense—as well as the relationship between these various forms and their environment. Hence it seems to follow naturally that economics be included in sociobiology, agreeing with Marshall's assertion, in his *Principles of Eco-*

nomics, that "economics has no near kinship with any physical science. It is a branch of biology broadly interpreted."[1] At this stage I confine myself to the similarities and leave the discussion of the more general question of sociobiology and its many implications to the end of this book.

I first show how some analyses of enterprise and industry have been carried out in the framework of a more or less automatic adjustment mechanism, excluding consideration of strategies. The presentation of certain simple mechanical models used in biology will then allow me to widen the scope of this kind of analogy.

2.1 Profit Maximization and Natural Selection

One of the principal reasons advanced to defend the neoclassical theory that firms maximize their profits is that the forces of competition automatically eliminate those firms that do not pursue this objective.[2]

Thus, according to Friedman (1953, pp. 19–23), even if firms do not really carry out marginal evaluations in their search for profit, the only ones to survive in the long run will be those whose decisions are compatible with neoclassical theory. In connection with this, Friedman presents his famous comparison to the snooker player. He asserts that the behavior of those enterprises that survive in the long run can be predicted by a theory of profit maximization just as the behavior of a snooker champion can be predicted by assuming that the player is capable of solving the corresponding mathematical problem. But as Koopmans (1957, p. 140) notes, if the argument of natural selection is the basis for our belief in profit maximization, "then we should postulate that basis itself and not the profit maximization which it implies in certain circumstances."[3] In any case this kind of approach was first developed by

Alchian (1950), who started by noting that under uncertainty, profit maximization is not a well-defined criterion. Whether the problem is one of imperfect and costly information or one of the inability of the human mind to resolve complex problems because of limited rationality, the existence of uncertainty implies that to each action corresponds not a unique outcome but a distribution of potential outcomes. It is, then, not possible to determine in a general way which is the best distribution.

For example, assume that there are only two possible actions: The outcome of the first is a high expected profit accompanied by a high variance, including the risk of bankruptcy; the other corresponds to a lower expected profit but also a lower variance. For the producers in this situation there is no single decision criterion: Either one action or the other will rationally be chosen according to the existence or nonexistence of risk aversion.[4] Alchian resolves the issue by affirming that, even if individual agents do not know precisely their costs, or revenues, and behave randomly, the decisions that emerge ex post as the correct ones among all possible decisions will be directly related to the realized positive profits necessary for survival.

Like the biologist, the economist predicts the effects of environmental changes on the surviving class of living organisms; the economist need not assume that each participant is aware of, or acts according to, his costs and demand situation. (Alchian 1950, p. 221)

In this context modes of behavior replace the rules determined by equilibrium conditions, and the insistence on ex post positive profits substitutes for the requirement of maximum profits. We can then envisage various forms of pondered adaptive behavior. Thus imitating profitable enterprises is an important step. It may take the form of adopting the going representative rules on "mark-up," financial ratios, and advertising. It must be stressed, however, that none of these actions ensures convergence to some maximum. In fact, in an uncertain and changing world it cannot be postulated that the producer is able to classify clearly a trial as a success or a failure or that there is a continuous tendency toward increasingly favorable results.

Nevertheless Alchian seems to refer to some optimization process when he states that

among all competitors, those whose particular conditions happen to be the most appropriate of those offered to the economic system for testing and adoption will be selected as survivors. (1950, p. 213)

Enke (1951) takes the survival argument even further. He considers that, although the firm, which has incomplete information on hand, subjectively perceives the outcome of each possible action as uncertain, this outcome is nevertheless objectively determined. There exists an objectively optimal behavior that would be followed if information were complete but is in any case adopted through the intensity of competitive pressure: Given that successful competitive firms grow and absorb an increasing share of the market, the minimum threshold of survival must tend to increase over time in such a way that in the long run *viability requires optimality.* Once again the economist may rightly make the assumption that in the long run firms behave "as if they were optimizing," even if they are not conscious of it.

Among the various criticisms of these approaches,[5] the fundamental one concerns the hypothesis of a process that is basically independent of individuals' motives but that can ensure convergence to a state in which only the most profitable survive. In fact, the mechanism of this dynamic evolution is not analyzed in any way and is far from being easily identified. For instance, the acquisition of resources

allowing growth does not happen instantaneously, and
some period of time must elapse before greater profitability
of firms approximating optimal behavior is reflected in
their higher share in economic activity. There is, however,
no a priori reason why firms should behave in a coherent
manner over time. Those who at a given moment adopt a
behavior consistent with profit maximization do not necessarily adopt the same kind of behavior in subsequent periods. If in each period behavior is purely random, the
market cannot tend to select profit-maximizing firms as the
survivors, because there is no firm that will adopt this
behavior persistently; by definition, there is no correlation
between performances in two different time periods. If on
the other hand behavior is based on "usual" reactions,
then it is accepted that firms whose usual behavior is consistent with profit maximization will grow relative to other
firms in the economy. As a consequence of this relative
expansion, we should expect a change in the price system,
leading to a new economic environment for all firms.
Again, there is no a priori reason in this modified environment for the same firms following the same routines to act
in a way that is more consistent with profit maximization
than their competitors. Thus, although a classification of
firms according to their affinity to profit-maximizing behavior requires particular environmental conditions, the
dynamic process itself changes this environment and calls
for a change in the behavior of firms.

A recent model developed by Chiappori (1984) confirms
these criticisms. The starting point is the following dilemma: Either the natural selection argument is explicitly
based on the assumption that a firm optimizing at a given
moment will continue to do so in the future, or one accepts
that an enterprise optimizing at a given moment may cease
to do so at another time. The first case implies that the firm
resorts intentionally to a process allowing it to attain its

optimum at all times, which is precisely what the support-
ers of natural selection theory claim they are not obliged to
assume. In the second case, one can show that firms that
are nonoptimizers do not disappear in equilibrium.

In order to show this inconsistency, Chiappori considered an economy in which two types of firms coexist, those
that optimize (O) and those that do not (S). At any given
time, each firm is defined by its size n. The model exam-
ines the random walk of a cohort of firms over a set of
states $O_1, \ldots, O_n$ and $S_1, \ldots, S_n$, where the O_i (or S_i)
define the state of the optimizing (or nonoptimizing) firm
of size i. The selection mechanism is expressed in terms of
strictly positive probabilities of passage from one state to
another, where P is the probability of growth (from O_n to
O_{n+1}), Q is the probability of decline (from S_n to S_{n-1}), π is
the probability of degeneracy (from O_n to S_n), and μ is the
probability of improvement (from S_n to O_n). Assuming a
Markov process, Chiappori showed that a significant proportion of nonoptimizing firms of all possible sizes remains
in the economy.[6]

The only way to escape the dilemma, therefore, is either
to explain certain organizational characteristics of the enterprise likely to ensure the transmission over time of the
optimizing behavior or to keep the maximization postulate
as it stands. The first approach comes under recent theories on the organization of the enterprise, which is examined in chapter 5.[7] Among those economists following the
second approach, some shift the role of natural selection
from individual behavior to the determination of a "natural" structure of industry in long-term equilibrium. These
recent contributions are reviewed in the next section.

2.2 Technological Determinism and Natural Market Structure

Because natural selection does not lead to maximizing behavior, one is forced to assume its existence. If one accepts
the hypothesis of profit maximization, then the possible
role of natural selection in our decentralized economies
will relate to competitive processes liable to ensure the
emergence of optimal market structures. The question
takes the following form: Do industries observed in long-
term equilibrium exhibit forms or structures dictated by
technological efficiency? This is asserted by many authors[8]
who believe that market forms emerge "naturally." For
instance, according to McGee (1974):

Apart from those industries dominated by State controls, there is
the strongest presumption that the existing structure is the
efficient structure. (p. 104)

Baumol and Fischer (1978) asserted with more qualification
that:

While it is not necessarily true that the least costly form of market
organisation will always prevail, it would be highly surprising if
there were not a rough correspondence between the most economic market form and what actually occurs. (p. 461)

More recently, Baumol (1982) confirmed this viewpoint in
presenting the theory of "contestable markets":

While the industry structures which emerge in reality are not
always those which minimise costs, they will constitute reasonable approximations to the efficient structure. (p. 8)

This approach is presented in two stages. First, for a given
industry and for all possible output vectors, the structure
of that industry corresponding to minimum costs will be
established (selection criterion). Second, the market process that can allow this industrial structure to emerge will
be defined (selection mechanism).

According to the authors cited, the selection criterion that determines an industry to be constituted as a natural monopoly, duopoly, or oligopoly is based simply on the relation between the firm's cost function and the given output vector. It is well known that, in an industry made up of firms producing a single output and using the same technology, if the long-run average cost function is U-shaped and has its unique minimum at a production level of, say, 1000 units per year while the industry is selling 5000 units per year, there can be exactly five efficient firms, each producing at the minimum of its average cost. More generally, for a given output level, the selection criterion is synonymous with a population of firms achieving this output at minimum cost.

A formal condition for this criterion to be satisfied is the notion of subadditivity of the cost function. For a total production level of $\bar{q}$, a cost function is called subadditive if the following inequality holds for all $q < \bar{q}$:

$$C(q) < C(x) + C(q - x), \qquad \forall x \text{ such that } 0 < x < q.$$

If $\bar{q}$ corresponds to the highest level of industrial demand, the given inequality implies that the industry should be a natural monopoly. As figure 2.1 illustrates, for average cost functions reaching their minimum at production levels q_0 and $2q_0$, we can see that for all demand $q < q_1$, where q_1 corresponds to the intersection of the two curves, we have subadditivity and therefore a natural monopoly.[9] On the other hand, for any output level $q > q_1$, two firms are more efficient than one, and for $q = 2q_0$ we should have a *natural duopoly*.

The following theorem can be proved more generally. Assume that all potential firms have access to the same technology and that all face the same input prices. Moreover, assume that the average cost function has a unique minimum at $q = q_0$ and is strictly decreasing in the open

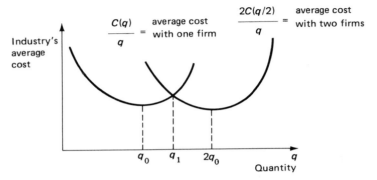

Figure 2.1
Average cost and efficient market structure.

interval $(0, q_0)$. The number of firms n that can produce the output of the industry $\bar{q}$ at minimum cost is then $n^* = \bar{q}/q_0$ when this ratio is a whole number.[10,11]

A sufficient condition for subadditivity is the existence of economies of scale.[12] A cost function C has global economies of scale at production level q if

$$C(\lambda q) < \lambda C(q)$$

for all λ, where $\lambda > 1$, $q \geq 0$. Dividing both sides of the inequality by λq, we obtain

$$\frac{C(\lambda q)}{\lambda q} < \frac{C(q)}{q}.$$

In other words, average costs are a decreasing function of output in the neighborhood of q. When a cost function is such that average costs are decreasing for all q, then it is strictly subadditive. Indeed, if $q > x$, then

$$\frac{C(x)}{x} > \frac{C(q)}{q} \quad \text{and} \quad \frac{C(q - x)}{q - x} > \frac{C(q)}{q}.$$

This implies that

$$C(x) + C(q - x) > C(q) \left(\frac{x}{q} + \frac{q - x}{q} \right) = C(q).$$

The situation in which firms jointly produce several goods is more complicated (Baumol et al. 1982). In the first place, it is not clear how economies of scale can be measured. One approach would be to define "baskets" of goods produced in fixed proportions. The sequence of various sizes of such baskets lies along an expansion path, amounting to a ray through the origin in the space of outputs. The behavior of average cost as well as the point where it attains its minimum may be defined along such a ray. Figure 2.2 illustrates a "ray average cost" (RAC) for a joint production of cars and trucks. It turns out that, when the goods are produced in the ratio set by the ray OR, average cost is minimized at output $y = y_0$.[13]

A second difficulty in the multiproduct case is that the existence of economies of scale, either for each product separately or along the expansion paths that hold outputs in fixed proportions, no longer ensures the subadditivity of

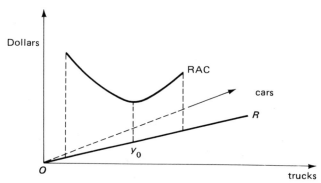

Figure 2.2
Ray average cost (RAC) and efficient scale.

the cost function. To illustrate this point, the cost function

$$C(q_1, q_2) = q_1 + q_2 + (q_1 q_2)^{1/3}$$

has economies of scale for each product. Indeed

$$\lambda C(q_1, q_2) = \lambda q_1 + \lambda q_2 + \lambda(q_1 q_2)^{1/3} >$$

$$\lambda q_1 + \lambda q_2 + (\lambda q_1 \lambda q_2)^{1/3} = \lambda q_1 + \lambda q_2 + \lambda^{2/3}(q_1 q_2)^{1/3}$$

$$= C(\lambda q_1, \lambda q_2),$$

where $\lambda > 1$. Nevertheless this function is not subadditive. In particular,

$$C(q_1, 0) + C(0, q_2) = q_1 + q_2 < C(q_1, q_2)$$
$$\text{for all } q_1 > 0 \text{ and } q_2 > 0.$$

This inequality expresses the existence of diseconomies in joint production that counterbalance the economies of scale and favor firms specializing in one product: There should therefore be no tendency in this case toward a natural monopoly of a multiproduct firm.

Let us now consider the case of economies of joint production. These "economies of scope" related to the production of a range of goods require for two products[14,15]

$$C(q_1, q_2) < C(q_1, 0) + C(0, q_2), \qquad q_1 > 0, q_2 > 0.$$

This phenomenon corresponds to some form of externality in the production of two (or many) goods, the existence of common costs, and certain indivisibilities. But in effect, for joint products, even the simultaneous presence of economies of scale and economies of scope is not a sufficient condition for subadditivity.[16] For my purpose the important point is that, even for multiproduct plants, it has been technically possible to define, given the output vector, the relation between technical efficiency requirements resulting from cost function parameters and the optimal number of firms in an industry. Market structure should be "naturally" concentrated when the output vector of the industry is small relative to the output vector that the firm must produce in order to minimize its costs. On the other hand, the larger the potential demand relative to the output of the cost-minimizing firm, the more decentralized the industry. Transformations in market structure over time will depend on the interaction between the growth in demand of the industry and the evolution of production techniques in that industry. For example, Novshek and Sonnenschein (1980) have shown that, when the optimal production scale tends to become insignificant relative to demand, a Cournot-Nash equilibrium can approximate a Walrasian equilibrium, defined by a continuum of price-taking firms of infinitesimal size.

Having thus examined the criterion for selection of the natural market structure, namely the minimization of production and organizational costs incurred in realizing a given output vector in this market, we must now consider the mechanism that ensures such a selection.

In a framework in which the population of firms remaining in long-run equilibrium is determined by the least costly market structure, it is important to define the selection mechanism liable to lead to this equilibrium. The competitive process is a priori bound to be the mainspring. If we limit ourselves to price competition, this process must ensure the equality between market prices and marginal costs in the long run.

One well-known adjustment mechanism is Walras's tâtonnement process, in which a vector of normalized prices $(p_1, p_2, \ldots, p_{n-1})$ is "called out at random" by an auctioneer and then modified so long as supply and demand are not equal. Because the conditions for perfect competition are satisfied, the competitive equilibrium is reached when net demand E_i, that is, the discrepancy between demand and supply of good i, is equal to zero in each market. This can be written as

$$E_i(p_1^*, p_2^*, \ldots, p_{n-1}^*) = 0 \qquad \text{for } i = 1, 2, \ldots, n - 1,$$

where the p_i^* are the equilibrium prices.

Note that, although Walras's tâtonnement process is often advanced as the solution to a system of simultaneous equations in a corresponding number of unknowns, it leaves unresolved the question of the adjustment process over time, the convergence and the speed of convergence of successive adjustments toward an equilibrium.

In the last few years efforts to refine the Walrasian tâtonnement have increased greatly,[17] in particular by abandoning certain features of perfect competition, such as perfect flexibility of prices and perfect information on the part of transactors. Nevertheless the fundamental objection to competitive equilibrium is that its conditions are not and cannot be fulfilled in most markets.

Walras himself mentioned an alternative (or complementary) adjustment process, namely, the mechanism of entry and exit.

If the selling price of a good is higher than the cost of the productive services to some firms, and a profit is realised as a result, entrepreneurs will congregate towards this branch of production or will increase their output, such that the quantity of the product will increase, its price will decrease, and the difference between price and cost will be reduced. (Walras 1874–1877)

He describes a similar adjustment through exit, when cost is higher than selling price for some firms. In fact, the phenomenon of entry and exit has been recognized as an adjustment process at least since Adam Smith and is viewed as a long-term regulator. In the framework of partial equilibrium analysis, it is precisely the use of this kind of adjustment that allows Baumol et al. (1982) to show not only that the endogenous determination of industrial structure can be compatible with the selection criterion discussed previously but also that this correspondence is obtained by abandoning the particularly restrictive requirement in perfect competition of the absence of important economies of scale. Their theory is based on the concept of a *perfectly contestable market*. The potential entrants in this market possess two properties. First, they must be able to serve without any restriction the same market demand, and they must employ the same production techniques that are accessible to the incumbent firms; this ensures that the potential entrants are not subject to any cost disadvantage. Second, the entrants must assess the profitability of entry on the basis of prices obtained before entry by incumbent firms.

More generally, entry is free because potential competitors have the same cost functions and can enter and exit without capital loss during the time taken by incumbent firms to change prices. In a sense, "the theory replaces price-taking with rapid entry and exit" (Spence 1983, p. 982). To characterize an *equilibrium configuration in a perfectly contestable market*, several successively nested conditions are therefore essential.[18]

The configuration of an industry $(m, q_1, \ldots, q_m, p)$ is called *feasible* if the m firms in the industry produce output levels of $q_1, \ldots, q_m$ at a nonnegative price p in such a way that the market equates supply and demand, $\Sigma_{i=1}^{m} q_i = Q(p)$, and each firm at least covers its production costs, $pq_i - C(q_i) \geq 0, i = 1, \ldots, m$. This industrial configuration will be a monopoly if $m = 1$, competitive if m is sufficiently large, and oligopolistic for intermediate values of m.

A feasible industrial configuration with price p and firm outputs $q_1, \ldots, q_m$ is called *sustainable* if it offers no possibility of profitable entry, that is, if $p_e q_e \leq C(q_e)$ for all $p_e \leq p$ and $q_e \leq Q(p_e)$, which are positive. In other words, under the assumption that the prices at which incumbent firms operate are not changed after entry, the entrant has no feasible plan of action that will guarantee positive profits.

The following result is then established: In a *perfectly contestable market*, equilibrium can be formed only by a sustainable (and of course feasible) industrial configuration. The reason is clear. If the configuration were not sustainable, it would be worthwhile for some entrepreneurs to enter without costs and extract some profits. The configuration would then change, either by the entry of new firms or by certain price reactions or any other measure to reject the new entrants. Even if these measures were applied, however, the entrants would still extract temporary profits by raiding the industry. Given that equilibrium requires the absence of new entrants, an equilibrium configuration in a perfectly contestable market must not offer any incitement to entry and hence must be sustainable.

In a perfectly contestable market, equilibrium has particularly rich properties. Three aspects may be emphasized. First, the selection criterion, that is, the minimization of total costs of the industry, is satisfied. Neither a different number of firms nor a different distribution of size or of production can produce the required industrial output at a cost lower than the existing feasible and sustainable configuration. The formal proof, which is obtained by contradiction, has the following intuitive basis: Given that no firm operates at a loss in the existing configuration, any group of firms forming an alternative industrial configuration that could produce the same total output at lower cost would globally make positive profits at existing prices. Hence at least one firm of this alternative configuration would make positive profits at the given prices; it could therefore begin profitable operations within the existing configuration by doing what it would in the alternative

configuration. The initial configuration would therefore
not be sustainable.

A second property is that, if there are at least two firms
in the industry, no good can be sold at a price different
from marginal cost. Let me clarify this point. If a firm sells q
units of output at a price p below marginal cost, then without making losses, $\pi \geq 0$, it is possible for an entrant to
supply a slightly lower output, $q - \varepsilon$, and still make a
profit. Because the price p is less than marginal cost, selling
$q - \varepsilon$ units of output at price p must in fact bring a profit
equal to $\pi + \varepsilon(Cm - p) > 0$, where π is the profit made
when selling q units at price p and Cm denotes marginal
cost. Therefore there must be a price just below p that
allows the entrant to undercut the incumbent firm while
still making as much profit as the incumbent by eliminating the marginal nonprofitable unit of production. Conversely, price cannot be above marginal cost when there
are at least two incumbent firms. Otherwise the possibility
of profitable entry would again arise. With two firms the
entrant can sell at a slightly lower price, attract the custom-
ers of firm 1, and moreover take ε units from firm 2. If
firms 1 and 2 sell together, $q_1 + q_2 > q_1$, the entrant can
attract a total purchase of $q_1 + \varepsilon > q_1$ for a sufficiently small
ε and make on this an extra profit of $\varepsilon(p - Cm) > 0$. The
presence of a second firm is necessary, however, to guar-
antee that the entrant can sell more than firm 1 without
a substantial reduction in price.[19]

Finally, it is clear that if $pq_i < C(q_i)$ for an established firm
i, the industrial configuration of which it is a member is not
feasible, and if $pq_i > C(q_i)$, this configuration is not sustainable because an entrant can sell at a lower price and still
make a profit. A feasible and sustainable configuration
therefore requires that $pq_i = C(q_i)$ for all its members i.

We then get the following remarkable result: Even in a
duopoly, price, average cost, and marginal cost must be
equal at equilibrium, as is required of a first-order op-

timum. In this sense the notion of a perfectly contestable equilibrium is a generalization of the perfectly competitive equilibrium. On the one hand, a long-run competitive equilibrium is a sustainable industrial configuration,[20] such that a perfectly competitive market is a perfectly contestable market. On the other hand, a perfectly contestable equilibrium does not require a large number of firms in the market and includes the case in which technology has important returns to scale.

This model of a selection process based on a criterion of technological efficiency, although of great interest, rests on particularly unreasonable assumptions, rendering the assertion of a close relationship between "natural" and actual market structures rather hazardous.

In the first instance technology plays the essential part, whereas demand seems to determine only the size of the industry. Therefore such phenomena as product differentiation, either by quality or by region, and monopolistic competition are excluded. Demand responds to price differences with a lag, which must be shorter than the lag required for incumbents to change prices,[21] so that profitable selling and exit can occur before existing firms respond.[22]

Second, there is complete symmetry between entrants and established firms as well as among the incumbents themselves. Technological differences, the existence of irreversible investments, material or otherwise, and the resulting asymmetry over time are totally ignored. Equally, the analysis ignores the role of uncertainty[23] and of incomplete information, where the firm does not know its opponents' preferences and strategies.

Finally, even in the framework of competition among a small number of firms, the economic analysis remains "impersonal," constraints are "natural" and impose themselves on the agent; there is no explicit strategic behavior, such as bluffing, dissuasion, credible threats, and irreversible commitments through irretrievable expenditure and more generally for the manipulation of environmental conditions and rules of the game. In fact, the rules of the game and the strategy spaces of incumbents and potential entrants are not clearly defined,[24] although equilibrium outcome critically depends on them.

A different reading of the industrial universe could in fact throw some light on the role of these latter phenomena and raise doubts on any long-run tendency to attain the "Pangloss" equilibrium. Before taking up this viewpoint, however, it is useful to present biological models that are similar to the mechanistic approach of the previous sections and that suggest the possible extension of analogies, in particular at the interindustry level.

2.3 Biological Interactions and Survival Mechanisms

In mathematical biology mechanical models aimed at representing the law of evolution of a population or of many interacting populations are old. Undoubtedly the most famous is that arising from the works of Malthus, who had a great influence on Darwin. A traditional presentation is as follows. Define by $N = N(t)$ the total population of a country at time t, and assume that births and deaths are constant proportions α and β of the size of the population and of the short time interval considered δt; the growth in population δN in this interval can be written

$$\delta N = \alpha N \, \delta t - \beta N \, \delta t = \gamma N \, \delta t,$$

where $\gamma = \alpha - \beta$. By dividing by δt and taking the limits as $\delta t \to 0$, we obtain a differential equation corresponding to the law of Malthus:

$$dN/dt = \gamma N. \tag{2.1}$$

Because the solution of this equation implies an exponential growth of N for $\gamma > 0$,[25] Verhulst suggested the introduction of an upper limit $\bar{N}$ for the population such that a transformed equation (2.1) leads to more realistic conclusions. The new expression[26] is

$$dN/dt = \gamma N(1 - N/\bar{N}), \qquad (2.2)$$

and the stationary state $dN/dt = 0$ is obtained when $N = \bar{N}$.

Finally, this kind of logistic equation has been completed by various additional terms, expressing the interaction effects between populations. The best known system of differential equations is that of Lotka and Volterra, featuring relations of competition between species. When there are two species, the system is written

$$dN_1/dt = N_1(a - bN_1 - cN_2),$$

$$dN_2/dt = N_2(e - fN_1 - gN_2), \qquad (2.3)$$

where N_1 and N_2 are the population densities of the two species at time t and $a, b, c, e, f,$ and g are positive constants.[27]

Starting from these basic models, researchers have explored various interspecific (or "heterotypical") interactions.

If we limit ourselves to two species, we see that some relations are unfavorable to both species (competition), others favor both simultaneously (mutualism and cooperation), and others favor only one species, either at the expense of the other (parasitism) or not (commensalism). An example of mutualism is that of lichens, which are couplings of a fungus and an alga. Neither species can grow and survive without the other. A situation of commensalism is that of balanus, a shellfish living on the shells of sea mollusks. An example of parasitism (in which the parasite

Table 2.1
Principal relations between species[a]

Nature of interactions	Species in contact		Separated species	
	A	B	A	B
Competition	−	−	0	0
Predation or parasitism[b]	+	−	−	0
Symbiosis or mutualism	+	+	−	−
Cooperation	+	+	0	0
Commensalism[c]	+	0	−	0

a. + indicates favored species; −, disadvantaged species; 0, uninfluenced species.
b. Species A predator of species B.
c. Species A commensal to species B.

is often smaller than the host) is that of the tick, which becomes embedded in the skin of another animal to draw its blood. Finally, cooperation is the case in which the association of the species is not essential, but their union is advantageous to both; a typical example is that of herons and terns, who nest collectively in order to resist possible predators better. Table 2.1 shows the main interactions identified in biology and distinguishes the situation in which the species are in contact from that in which they live separately.

These various interactions can be illustrated graphically, and some analogies with economics can be found. In the partial equilibrium framework, figure 2.3 illustrates three types of interspecific equilibria for two species. Let N_1 and N_2 be the population sizes of species 1 and 2, respectively. With $\dot{N} \equiv dN/dt$, we can write

$$\dot{N}_1 = f_1(N_1, N_2), \qquad \dot{N}_2 = f_2(N_2, N_1).$$

When there is competition between the two species, $\partial \dot{N}_1 / \partial N_2 < 0$ and $\partial \dot{N}_2 / \partial \dot{N}_1 < 0$. Let us consider a possible case

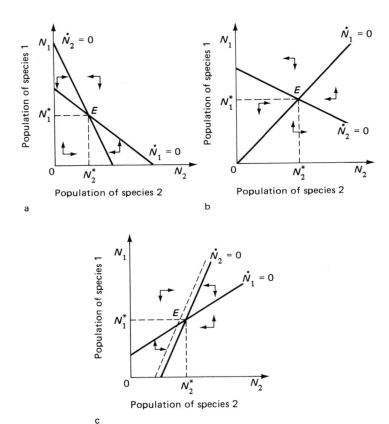

Figure 2.3
(a) Competition between species. (b) Predation between species.
(c) Mutualism between species.

(figure 2.3a). The two lines correspond to stationary states
of the population, that is, where both $\dot{N}_1$ and $\dot{N}_2$ are equal
to zero. The intersection of the two lines is an ecological
equilibrium. This equilibrium may or may not be stable. To
determine whether or not it is stable, we must examine the
direction of population changes for all points in the posi-

tive quadrant. The vectors in figure 2.3a indicate this direction. Thus, for any point above the line $\dot{N}_1 = 0$, $\dot{N}_1 < 0$; and for any point below, $\dot{N}_1 > 0$. By joining the vectors, we form a path in the form of a spiral converging to the stationary equilibrium. We have in this case a stable situation corresponding to the coexistence of the two species. Of course, stability is not always guaranteed, even in the linear case; in general, nonlinear relationships lead to an extremely wide range of possible dynamic behavior (Lotka 1956; Volterra 1931; and Boulding 1950, ch. 1). A simple example illustrates the idea. Consider the dynamic system given by $\dot{N} = N^2 + a$. If a is positive, there is no equilibrium. If a is equal to zero, equilibrium exists for $N^* = 0$. Finally, if a is negative, $\dot{N} = 0$ requires that $N^2 = a$, which corresponds to two equilibrium values, $N^* = -a^{0.5}$ and $N^* = +a^{0.5}$. Therefore a small change in the value of the parameter a (its passage through zero), leads to a radical change in the dynamic system. Zero is called the point of "catastrophe" for the system $\dot{N} = N^2 + a$.[28]

When there is predation (or parasitism), species 2 favors species 1, which negatively affects species 2. In figure 2.3b the predator's population is shown along the y axis and that of the prey along the x axis. Equilibrium is attained at the intersection of the lines, and again it will be stable or unstable depending on the slopes of the lines. If the system oscillates in an explosive way, the two species can become extinct, insofar as the number of prey remaining at a given moment of time becomes insufficient to ensure the survival of predators.

Finally, in the case of symbiosis or mutualism, such as the bucolic relation between bees and flowers, the situation illustrated in figure 2.3c shows that population growth in one species favors the growth of the other. The equilibrium shown in this figure is stable. Note that any deteriora-

tion in environment that would affect the position of any of
the species (leading to the shifting of one of the lines to the
left) will have an equally negative effect on the population
of the other species.

It is obviously possible to find various analogies between
these ecological equilibria and economic situations. Thus
the *product life cycle theory* supposes that, after an initial
period of rapid expansion of sales of a new product, a
phenomenon of progressive slowing emerges, expressing
a saturation of demand and an increase in the number of
substitutes. Logistic curves have been used to describe this
evolution in the case of chemical products, cars, and consumer durables, and the corresponding parameters have
been estimated. These analyses can be extended to the
evolution of sectors and industrial networks, taking into
account the main technological interdependencies existing
among industries. For his part, Feenstra (1980) has put
forward a biological model to explain *international trade* in
similar but differentiated products. He considered the interaction between "genetic" characteristics common to a
group of countries (tastes, level of income, fixed costs of
research and development) and the specific environment
of a country (factor endowment, infrastructure, social
habits, family structure). A given variety of products (the
"phenotype") would emerge from these interactions. Bilateral trade in this variety of products could then develop as
a result of diffusion of tastes backed by advertising.

Starting with the usual sequence of invention, innovation, and diffusion, various authors have also used
"epidemic" learning models to describe *diffusion processes of
innovation,* according to which a new product or process
presented exogenously to the industry comes into wide-
spread use as one producer after another adopts the innovation. These models are based on the assumption that

within a short period of time the proportion of nonadopters deciding to adopt a given process or product (the proportion of people catching the disease) is proportional to the proportion of firms already using it (the proportion of people with the disease). Hence innovations diffuse through industries roughly according to the S-shaped logistic curve.[29]

Questions regarding the population of firms and *industrial demography* can equally be tackled in terms of biological models. Thus the logistic model giving the stationary stable state of a population for a given technology and environment arises from the same perspective as in the previous section, where the population of firms is limited by the size of the market, coupled with the minimum size of a firm. At a time when knowledge of the conditions under which firms are created and multiply or exit seems essential to our economies in mutation, this is a domain that has been little analyzed.

Let me present another possible analogy. Processes of *division of labor* featuring some kind of complementarity are similar to forms of mutualism,[30] whereas exploitation of one social category by another may evoke predatory relations. More generally, competition plays an essential role in human society, as in animal societies, and the more similar the organisms in question and the more they try to occupy the same ecological "niche," the more intense the competition. On the other hand, various forms of differentiation and specialization are liable to favor cooperative behavior, and interspecific relations should a priori be less intensely competitive than intraspecific ones.

These analogies have compelled Hirshleifer (1977, p. 50) to say that "biological processes and mechanisms represent more general classes into which the economic ones fall as particular instances." It would nevertheless be illusory to believe that the richness of relations within our industrial societies can be reduced to automatic adjustment phenomena and simple mechanical laws.

Discretionary research and development programs intend not only to produce new products but also to prevent rivals from doing so. Systematic changes in the range of products offered, creation of alternative organizational forms, and, in general, strategic choices made by economic agents, private or public, constantly modify the parameters of the system of equations in such a way that ceilings are transitory, constraints shift, and stationary states of equilibrium are unstable or never attained.

In contrast to the theories presented in the first chapter, the object of the following chapters is therefore to advance alternative approaches in which the complexity of strategic relations is taken into account by resorting to other concepts and other methods of analysis.

Notes

1. See A. Marshall, *Principles of Economics* (1890). It must be recalled that Marshall is one of the founders of industrial economics. In his book he discusses, among other things, the role of economies of scale and the problem of compatibility between rising productivity and perfect competition. The term "industrial organization" had already appeared in the book *Economics of Industry* (1879), which Marshall wrote jointly with his wife.

2. See Klein and Leffer (1981), p. 364. This viewpoint is often shared by businessmen. Penrose (1952), for instance, mentions in her article a statement by John D. Rockefeller:

The growth of a large business is merely a survival of the fittest. . . . The American Beauty rose can be produced in the splendor and fragrance which brings cheer to its beholder only by sacrificing the early buds which grow around it. This is not an evil tendency in business. It is merely the working out of nature and a law of God.

3. Recently, Aumann (1985) has adopted a similar view about biological analogies. After saying that he finds it "somewhat surprising that our disciplines have any relation at all to real behaviour," he states that "homo rationalis can serve as a model for certain aspects of the behaviour of *homo sapiens*." And he adds: This is related to ideas in biology and evolution, in which the doctrine of survival of the fittest translates into maximising behaviour on the part of individual genes. We know that genes don't really maximise anything; but the phenomena we observe, or some of them, are nicely tied together by the hypothesis that they act as if they were maximising. Things are more complicated in the social sciences, first because decisions themselves are very complex, and second because non-maximising conduct is not as ruthlessly punished as in the jungle, but perhaps there is a similar trend. (p. 36)

4. This problem exists also in biology. Various theories of evolution consider the reproduction of the species, measured as the ratio of the number of descendants to the number of parents, as a main objective. In a situation of certainty the best adaptive behavior maximizes this ratio or even transfers to the descendants the characteristics that allow a high rate of reproduction. But, if each action were to generate a probability distribution, the interesting criterion would not necessarily be the highest expected rate of reproduction. An alternative would be to minimize the risk of extinction, that is, to adopt the course of action for which the probability of extinction is the lowest (maximin). This criterion could better represent differences of genetic origin in the morphological, physiological, and psychological characteristics of individuals of the same species. This polymorphism (which is contrary to the idea of a holotype) can be explained by the notion that the more a set is genetically polymorphic, the larger its horizon and the greater its chances of survival. I discuss this question in chapter 6.

5. See, in particular, Penrose (1952, 1953) and Winter (1964, 1971).

6. The results follow from certain assumptions on the probabilities of passage ($P + \pi \leq 1$, $Q + \mu \leq 1$ among others), as well as on the tails of the chain, in particular, the existence of an environment E made up of potential firms, in such a way that the appearance of a new firm is formally defined by the passage from E to O_1 with probability R and in such a way that a disappearance is

defined by the passage from S_1 to E with probability Q. One of the models under study suggests the following diagram:

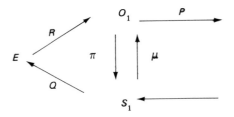

7. Note here the theory developed by Boulding (1950) on the basis of "homeostasis of the balance sheet." Starting from the notion in biology that a living organism faced with a changing external environment has at its disposal a set of mechanisms, such as the immune system, that allows it to maintain its internal conditions for life, Boulding applied this notion to the firm's balance sheet. As he emphasized, the homeostasis principle, however, says nothing about what determines and motivates the equilibrium:

In biology, it can generally be assumed that genetic constitution determines the state of equilibrium; in social organisms, however, the equilibrium position of the organism itself is to a considerable degree under the control of the organism's director. (1950, pp. 33–34)

See also Thorelli (1968) and Day (1975). As we will see, an approach allowing us to envisage the persistence of optimizing behavior over time could start from the analysis of organizational forms and decision procedures within the enterprise that last beyond momentary decisions and that are liable to provide "hereditary" transmission mechanisms.

8. See, for example, Weston and Lustgarten (1974), for whom technologies of industries are also at the root of concentration.

9. One particular cost function having the same shape as figure 2.1 is $C(q) = 1 + q^2$. When there is just one firm, the minimum average cost is obtained by setting

$$d\left[\frac{C(q)}{q}\right]\bigg/ dq = 0,$$

that is, $q_0 = 1$, whereas with two firms the minimum is obtained when

$$d\left[2C\left(\frac{q}{2}\right)\Big/q\right]\Big/dq = 0,$$

which implies $2q_0 = 2$. From the point of view of cost minimization, there will be indifference between production with one firm and production with two, at production level q_1 obtained such that

$$\frac{C(q)}{q} = \left[2C\left(\frac{q}{2}\right)\right]\Big/q,$$

which in this case implies

$$\frac{1 + q^2}{q} = \left[2\left(1 + \frac{q^2}{4}\right)\right]\Big/q \to 1 + q^2 = 2 + \frac{q^2}{2}$$

and hence $q_1 = \sqrt{2}$. See Sharkey (1982), whose main arguments are reproduced here.

10. It should be emphasized that the theorem does not specify the optimal way in which the output of a given industry should be allocated among the optimal number of firms. It would be wrong in any case to conclude that the optimal allocation would be an egalitarian one. See Baumol and Fischer (1978).

11. When the ratio is not a whole number, we have a problem. In fact, n^* will be either the integer just below $\bar{q}/q_0$ or the interger just above. It is therefore clear that, if the intersection between the industry's demand curve and its average cost curve is at an output level that is not a multiple of q_0, at least one firm in the industry will have to produce more or less than q_0 so that the theoretically most efficient solution will not be reached. One way to resolve the difficulty is to replace the assumption of a unique minimum for the average cost curves by the undoubtedly more reasonable assumption of a horizontal segment such that there exists a whole range of outputs for which average cost is minimized. The question then becomes one of uniqueness of the solution.

12. This, however, is not a necessary condition. As Sharkey (1982) points out, a cost function can be subadditive but have average costs increasing over a range of outputs.

13. One can formally define the RAC of a multiproduct plant. Choose a certain basket of products y_0 to serve as numeraire, and assume that it is normalized such that $\Sigma_{i=1}^{n} y_{0i} = 1$. Given a production intensity measured by the scalar $t > 0$, the output vector ty_0 and the RAC, expressed as a function of t, are related by

$RAC(t|y_0) = C(ty_0)/t$.

For a given y_0, the RAC decreases if $RAC(t|y_0)$ is a decreasing function of t.

14. For a discussion on economies related to the existence of many production plants, see Scherer et al. (1975).

15. "Economies of scope" correspond to subadditivity applied to a restricted set of output vectors. For joint products the function C is subadditive if $C(y) + C(y') \geqslant C(y + y')$ for all y and y'. On the other hand, the function has "economies of scope" if $C(y) + C(y') \geqslant C(y + y')$ for all output vectors such that, if $y_i > 0$, then $y_i' = 0$, and if $y_i' > 0$, then $y_i = 0$ for all i (disjoint output vectors). See Sharkey (1982, p. 66), Panzar and Willig (1981), and Willig (1979).

16. The sufficient condition depends on strong requirements on joint production, which have been analyzed by means of the notion of cost complementarity, namely, a situation in which the marginal cost for any output level decreases as this or any other output level is increased. Analysis has allowed the determination of the optimal output proportion that the firm should realize in order to exploit the economies of joint production (choice of the ray in figure 2.2). See Baumol et al. (1982) and Willig (1979).

17. See, in particular, the articles by Dreze (1975), Malinvaud (1977), and Benassy (1982) on equilibria with price rigidity and quantitative rationing. For an analysis of the relation between models of imperfect competition and the Arrow-Debreu model as well as the question of existence of equilibria, see Mas-Colell (1982) and Hart (1985).

18. I confine myself to the case of the uniproduct firm. For the multiproduct firm, see Baumol et al. (1982), ch. 5.

19. The presence of a second firm ensures the existence of an $\varepsilon > 0$ such that, if q is the level of market demand at the initial price p, the proposed output of the entrant can be sold at this price because $q_1 + \varepsilon < q_1 + q_2 \leqslant q$. On the contrary, when the established

firm is a monopoly, output and price are directly constrained by elasticity of demand. An attempt to enter and sell $q + \varepsilon$ rather than q could provoke a drastic reduction in price, ruling out the expected profit from entry. The extreme case is when demand is perfectly inelastic. See Baumol (1982).

20. On the other hand, a sustainable industrial configuration may not be a long-run competitive equilibrium. We can present a simple illustration of this point. Consider the following diagram:

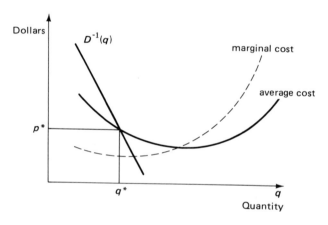

Here, the possible configuration has a single firm producing and selling q^* units at price p^*. This configuration is a *sustainable equilibrium* (a sustainable natural monopoly): Indeed, at a price less than or equal to p^*, the sale of any quantity on the demand curve (or to the right of this curve) corresponds to a revenue lower than cost, given that in this zone price is not above average cost. This configuration, however, is not a long-run competitive equilibrium; it is well known that, if the unique intersection between the demand curve and the average cost curve is situated in the zone of increasing returns, the long-run competitive equilibrium is in fact not feasible. Note that Bertrand's model also comes to the conclusion that in a duopoly in which the firms produce identical goods and compete on prices, equilibrium is achieved when price equals marginal cost. Contrary to the model developed by Baumol, Panzar, and Willig, this result depends on assumptions on the behavior of duopolists and not on that of the entrants.

Moreover, it is based on particular conditions on costs. This model is discussed in chapter 3.

21. Hence the theory rests on the assumption that price sustainability is the relevant equilibrium concept. Brock and Scheinkman (1983) have argued that quantity sustainability in which entrants enter on the expectation that incumbents' quantities, not prices, remain fixed is as plausible but does not have similar socially desirable properties.

22. According to Shepherd (1984), the assumptions of "ultrafree" entry are inconsistent. If entry is sufficiently negligible, it may indeed avoid a response. But because ultrafree entry must involve total (or at least significant) entry, thus leading to the optimal configuration, the nonresponse assumption is untenable.

23. In a recent article, Applebaum and Lim (1985) presented a model of a market that is characterized by uncertainty and that is ex post contestable. They showed that the incumbent will face a tradeoff between efficiency and flexibility and will generally make some commitments to take advantage of efficient ex ante technologies.

24. This aspect is discussed in Brock (1983).

25. Equation (2.1) can be written $(1/N)\,(dN/dt) = \gamma$. By integrating both sides with respect to t and after transformation, we obtain the solution for N:

$$N = N_0 e^{\gamma t},$$

where $N = N_0$ at $t = 0$.

26. Equation (2.2) is rewritten as

$$(dN/dt)/[N(1 - N/\bar{N})] = \gamma.$$

By integrating both sides, we get the solution

$$N = \bar{N}/[1 + ((\bar{N}/N_0) - 1)e^{-\gamma t}].$$

Verhulst's logistic equation implies a sigmoid evolution: The initial population $N_0 < \bar{N}$ would first increase exponentially; then for larger N, growth will be smaller, with $dN/dt \to 0$ as $N \to \bar{N}$.

27. One of the four stationary equations is the solution of $N_1 = e/f - (g/f)N_2$ and $N_2 = a/c - (b/c)N_1$, which, if $bg - cf \neq 0$, is given by

$$\left(\frac{ag - bc}{bg - cf},\ \frac{eb - af}{bg - cf} \right).$$

43

If we assume that $a/b < e/f$ and that $e/g < a/c$, then equilibrium is
stable. This situation corresponds to figure 2.3.

28. For an overview, see May (1976). In economics it has been
only recently that the analysis of deterministic nonlinear systems
has allowed the revival of traditional perspectives. It has thus
been possible to explain the endogenous emergence of cycles
(Grandmont 1985) and the emergence of "chaos" in economic
growth processes (Day 1983).

29. For an early work, see Mansfield (1968). A useful survey and
new developments are found in Davies (1979). See also Waterson
(1984), ch. 8.

30. Contrary to Houthakker (1956), Hirshleifer (1977, p. 35) carefully distinguishes the "competitive" division of labor from the
"cooperative" division of labor. In the first case competition is
mitigated by the subdivision of ecological niches and separation
of species; Hirshleifer compares it to monopolistic competition
and to differentiation according to locality. In the second case
there is development of complementarity between species, with
or without a common genetic basis; the analogy in economics is
such experiences as Taylorism and various forms of specialization. See Ghiselin (1974) for the biological aspect. This question is
related to the whole debate on the sources of altruism, which I
return to in chapter 6.

References

A. Alchian. 1950. "Uncertainty, evolution, and economic theory." *Journal of Political Economy* 58:211–221.

E. Applebaum and C. Lim. 1985. "Contestable markets under
uncertainty." *Rand Journal of Economics* 1:28–40.

R. Aumann. 1985. "What is game theory trying to accomplish?"
in *Frontiers of Economics*, K. Arrow and S. Honkapohja (eds.).
London: Blackwell, 28–76.

W. Baumol. 1982. "Contestable markets: An uprising in the theory of industry structure." *American Economic Review* 72(1):1–15.

W. Baumol and D. Fischer. 1978. "Cost minimizing number of
firms and determination of industry structure." *Quarterly Journal
of Economics* 92(3):439–467.

W. Baumol, J. Panzar, and R. Willig. 1982. *Contestable Markets and the Theory of Industry Structure.* San Diego: Harcourt Brace Jovanovich.

J. Benassy. 1982. *The Economics of Market Disequilibrium.* New York: Academic Press.

J. Bhagwati (ed.). 1982. *Import Competition and Response.* Chicago: University of Chicago Press.

K. Boulding. 1950. *A Reconstruction of Economics.* New York: Wiley.

W. Brock. 1983. "Contestable markets and the theory of industry structure: A review article." *Journal of Political Economy* 91(6):1055–1066.

W. Brock and J. Scheinkman. 1983. "Free entry and the sustainability of natural monopoly: Bertrand revisited by Cournot," in *Breaking up Bell,* D. Evans (ed.). Amsterdam: North-Holland, 150–175.

P. A. Chiappori. 1984. "Sélection naturelle et rationalité absolue des entreprises" (Natural selection and absolute rationality of firms). *Revue Economique* 1:87–107.

S. Davies. 1979. *The Diffusion of Process Innovations.* Cambridge: Cambridge University Press.

R. Day. 1975. "Adaptive processes and economic theory," in *Adaptive Economic Models,* R. Day and T. Graves (eds.). New York: Academic Press, 1–38.

R. Day. 1983. "The emergence of chaos from classical economic growth." *Quarterly Journal of Economics* 98(2):201–213.

J. Dreze. 1975. "Existence of and exchange equilibrium under price rigidities." *International Economic Review* 16(2):301–320.

J. Elster. 1979. *Ulysses and the Sirens: Studies in Rationality and Irrationality.* Paris: Edition de la Maison des Sciences de l'Homme.

S. Enke. 1951. "On maximizing profits: A distinction between Chamberlin and Robinson." *American Economic Review* 41:566–578.

R. Feenstra. 1980. "Product creation and trade patterns: A theoretical note on the 'biological' model of trade in similar products," in *Import Competition and Response*, J. Bhagwati (ed.). Chicago: University of Chicago Press, 184–195.

M. Friedman. 1953. *Essays in Positive Economics*. Chicago: University of Chicago Press.

M. Ghiselin. 1974. *The Economy of Nature and the Evolution of Sex*. Berkeley: University of California Press.

J. M. Grandmont. 1985. "On endogenous competitive business cycles." *Econometrica* 53(5):995–1045.

O. Hart. 1985. "Imperfect competition in general equilibrium: An overview of recent work," in *Frontiers of Economics*, K. Arrow and S. Honkapohja (eds.). London: Blackwell, 100–149.

J. Hirshleifer. 1977. "Economics from a biological point of view." *Journal of Law and Economics* 20(1):1–52.

H. Houthakker. 1956. "Economics and biology: Specialization and speciation." *Kyklos* 9:180–200.

B. Klein and K. Leffer. 1981. "The role of market performance in assuming contractual performance." *Journal of Political Economy* 89(4):615–641.

T. Koopmans. 1957. *Three Essays on the State of Economic Science*. New York: McGraw Hill.

A. Lotka. 1924. *Elements of Mathematical Biology*. New York: Dover. Reprinted 1956.

E. Malinvaud. 1977. *The Theory of Unemployment Reconsidered*. Oxford: Blackwell.

E. Mansfield. 1968. *Industrial Research and Technological Innovation*. London: Norton.

A. Marshall. 1890. *Principles of Economics*. London: Macmillan.

A. Marshall and M. P. Marshall. 1879. *Economics of Industry*. London: Macmillan.

A. Mas-Colell. 1982. *Non-cooperative Approach to the Theory of Perfect Competition*. New York: Academic Press.

R. M. May. 1976. "Simple mathematical models with very complicated dynamics." *Nature* 261:459–467.

J. McGee. 1974. "Efficiency and economies of size," in *Industrial Concentration: The New Learning*, H. Goldschmid, H. Mann, and J. Weston (eds.). Boston: Little, Brown, 55–97.

W. Novshek and H. Sonnenschein. 1980. "Cournot equilibrium with free entry." *Review of Economic Studies* 47:473–486.

J. Panzar, and R. Willig. 1981. "Economies of scope." *American Economic Review* 71(2):268–272.

E. Penrose. 1952. "Biological analogies in the theory of the firm." *American Economic Review* 5:804–819.

E. Penrose. 1953. "Communication." *American Economic Review* 4:603–609.

F. Scherer et al. 1975. *The Economics of Multi-plant Operation: An International Comparison Study*. Cambridge: Harvard University Press.

W. Sharkey. 1982. *The Theory of Natural Monopoly*. Cambridge: Cambridge University Press.

W. Shepherd. 1984. "Contestability vs. competition." *American Economic Review* 74(4):572–587.

M. Spence. 1983. "Contestable markets and the theory of industry structure: A review article." *Journal of Economic Literature* 21(3):981–990.

H. Thorelli. 1968. "Organizational theory: An ecological view." *Proceedings of the 27th Annual Conference of the Academy of Management*. Washington, D.C.: Academy of Management, 66–84.

V. Volterra. 1931. *Leçons sur la théorie mathématique de la lutte pour la vie* (Lessons in the mathematical theory of the struggle for life). Paris: Seuil.

L. Walras. 1874–1877. *Eléments d'économie pure* (Elements of pure economics). Lausanne: Corbas.

M. Waterson. 1984. *Economic Theory of Industry*. Cambridge: Cambridge University Press.

J. Weston and S. Lustgarten. 1974. "Concentration and wage-price changes," in *Industrial Concentration: The New Learning*, H. Goldschmid, H. Mann, and J. Weston (eds.). Boston: Little, Brown, 307–332.

R. Willig. 1979. "Multi-product technology and market structure." *American Economic Review* 9(2):346–356.

E. Wilson. 1975. *Sociobiology*. Cambridge: Harvard University
Press.

S. Winter. 1964. "Economic natural selection and the theory of
the firm." *Yale Economic Essays* 4:225–272.

S. Winter. 1971. "Satisficing, selection, and the innovating rem-
nant." *Quarterly Journal of Economics* 85(2):237–261.

3   Oligopolies and Market Power

The work discussed in the second chapter considered aspects of markets that lead by various selective mechanisms to a competitive equilibrium. In this chapter I concentrate on models for which the characteristics of the industry and the strategic behavior of economic agents lead to industrial configurations of equilibrium that are explained not by considerations of technical efficiency but by the pursuit of advantages linked to market power.

One of the most important foundations of the competitive model that is put into question by theories of imperfect competition is that, in order to be considered as price takers, the number of agents needs to be sufficiently large. In contrast, a situation of oligopoly, in which a small number of firms faces a large number of buyers, implies a strategic interdependence between sellers, such that the best policy for a firm will depend on that followed by each of its competitors. In this context the anonymity of competition disappears, and economic agents become players.

I first discuss the characteristics of the degree of concentration as a means of expressing the oligopolistic nature of a market; then I examine some simple models. In the Cournot- and Bertrand-type models, the firm has at its disposal decision variables, in price and/or in quantity, that it could not control in the competitive model; in this sense these models constitute the foundations of "strategic models." Nevertheless the strategy space of these models is limited, and, furthermore, the concept of equilibrium used is based on the hypothesis that the firm considers the behavior of its competitors as given. The essence of strategic models, however, is that economic agents are assumed to be able to take positions, both financially and psychologically, so as to discourage and to constrain the actions and reactions of their actual and potential rivals; they modify the expectations of others in a credible manner through their own commitments, which may be irrevocable or simply perceived as such. In this perspective I show in sections 3.2 and 3.3 by means of a critical discussion of the concept of rational conjectural variation the need to go beyond both a static framework of analysis and Nash's concept of equilibrium. Finally, in section 3.4 I introduce recent approaches in biology that, contrary to those of the previous chapter, transcend the mechanical processes of selection and present concepts of equilibrium analogous to those used in models of imperfect competition.

Before starting the first section, it should be recalled that the evaluation of the existing degree of monopoly within a market clearly requires a number of aspects to be taken into account, including not only the degree of concentration but also the characteristics of the product, organizational form, barriers to entry and exit, changes in demand, and technological innovation. Only a real "balance sheet" of market structure, firms' behavior, and realized performance will allow in a concrete case a well-founded appreciation.[1] Instead of proposing general ideas on this matter, the consistency of which is often questionable, an increasing number of researchers is trying to present a rigorous analysis of these characteristics, with varying degrees of success. Within the framework of a primarily theoretical debate, I use this type of work to clarify the discussion.

3.1 Degree of Concentration and Value Judgments

Indexes of concentration have generally been analyzed as instruments of measure that differ only in their statistical properties. In this section I explain this aspect but stress the fact that the adoption of a particular measure must equally involve a value judgment.

For a given industry, defined as a set of firms producing the same good, an index of concentration characterizes this industry on the basis of the number of firms n and of the distribution of their more or less unequal market shares $m = (m_1, \ldots, m_n)$, where $m_i \geqslant 0$, $i = 1, \ldots, n$, and $\Sigma_{i=1}^{n} m_i = 1$.

If $F(m_1, \ldots, m_n)$ is a cardinal representation of concentration, a certain number of desirable properties will be satisfied if the function F is symmetric and strictly convex:[2] For example, concentration must increase if one firm's market share grows at the expense of a smaller firm's (transfer principle), and a merger should also increase concentration. Nevertheless the set of properties usually studied in the literature will, at most, allow us to restrict the families of indexes that should be taken into consideration. Among these, families of additively separable functions of the following form are generally considered:

$$F(m_1, \ldots, m_n) = \sum_{i=1}^{n} m_i h(m_i),$$

where $h(m_i)$ represents a numerical function defined in [0, 1], expressing the weight given to a firm with market share m_i. More specifically, Hannah and Kay (1977) have suggested the following weighting function:

$$h(m_i) = m_i^{\theta - 1} \quad \text{for } \theta > 0 \text{ and } \neq 1.$$

The corresponding family of indexes of concentration is then written

$$F_\theta(m_1, \ldots, m_n) = \sum_{i=1}^{n} m_i^\theta.$$

In order to define the principal indexes of concentration usually employed, one simply needs to choose a particular value for the parameter θ. Thus, for $\theta = 2$, Herfindhal's index is obtained:[3]

$$F_2(m_1, \ldots, m_n) = \Sigma\, m_i^2 = H,$$

that is, the sum of the squares of the market shares. The equivalent number associated with this is expressed by

$$f_2(m_1, \ldots, m_n) = \left(\sum_{i=1}^{n} m_i^2 \right)^{\frac{1}{1-2}} = \frac{1}{H},$$

or the inverse of Herfindhal's index.

For $\theta = 1$, the index is not defined; but, by letting the order in the general entropy formula[4] tend to unity, we obtain the measure proposed by Theil (1967) as the inverse of the degree of concentration:

$$E = \sum_{i=1}^{n} m_i \ln \frac{1}{m_i} = -\sum_{i=1}^{n} m_i \ln m_i.$$

Note that in information theory and in thermodynamics this entropy is a quantitative measure of uncertainty expressed by a probability distribution (Shannon 1948). It is at its largest for a uniform distribution (in this case, for an equal distribution of market shares, $E = \ln n$), because this implies that there is little or no specific information available.[5] It is equal to zero ($E = 0$) when the system is in a specific state with certainty (in this case, a situation of monopoly). The entropy measure of concentration, in the form of a direct measure, is then written

$$C_E = \Sigma \, m_i \ln m_i,$$

which varies from $-\ln n$ to 0.

An interesting property of this index is additivity. Assume that the set of n firms on the market is arranged in s mutually exclusive categories, denoted by S_t ($t = 1, \ldots, s$) (for example, on the basis of the type of control exerted on the firms—public, private, national, international, financial). The entropy measure of concentration can then be disaggregated in such a way that it can be expressed as

$$C_E = \sum_{i=1}^{m} m_i \ln m_i = \sum_{t=1}^{s} \sum_{i \in S_t} m_i \left(\ln \frac{m_i}{m_t} + \ln m_t \right)$$

$$= \sum_{t=1}^{s} m_t \left(\sum_{i \in S_t} \frac{m_i}{m_t} \ln \frac{m_i}{m_t} + \ln m_t \right).$$

The expression

$$\sum_{i \in S_t} \frac{m_i}{m_t} \ln \frac{m_i}{m_t}$$

denotes the value of the entropy measure of concentration C_{E_t} within the group S_t. The expression $\Sigma_{t=1}^{s} m_t \ln m_t$ corresponds to the intergroup entropy measure of concentration C_{E_L} (concentration on the basis of the groups' market shares).

Hence the global concentration for n firms is written[6]

$$C_E = \sum_{t=1}^{s} m_t \, C_{E_t} + C_{E_L}.$$

If this additivity property is ignored, however, the choice of a value for the parameter θ or for the function $h(m_i)$ is a subjective one. For instance, choosing $\theta = 2$

implies that in measuring the concentration we are giving a proportionally higher weight to large firms, whereas choosing $\theta \rightarrow 1$ assumes that we wish to decrease this weight. Consequently, Herfindhal's measure amplifies the importance of large firms, whereas Theil's entropy measure reduces it. At this stage there is no axiomatic basis for such a choice (see, however, d'Aspremont et al. (1986)). It would have to be dictated by economic policy considerations. For instance, in measuring the existing degree of concentration in a given industry, a government might give a low weight to the market shares of public enterprises while assuming a higher weight for subsidiaries of foreign multinationals.

The important point is that the necessity to make this choice contradicts those who would like to see in the adoption of a particular measure of concentration a selection based solely on statistical properties, to the exclusion of any normative judgment.

In examining quantity and price oligopoly models, we can also see that the type of conduct attributed to firms influences the measure of the degree of concentration, because this degree not only is set by technological conditions but also depends on the adopted concept of solution and on the assumed expectations.

3.2 Oligopolies and Quantity Competition

Some authors, for example, Demsetz (1974), suggest that there is no theoretical analysis that establishes a general link between concentration indexes and monopoly power without making special assumptions about entry conditions. For various static and dynamic models of oligopolistic competition, however, most of the measures of concentration including the entropy measure do have a direct relationship with the degree of monopoly. This section is devoted to Cournot-type models, whereas the next section focuses on price oligopolies, and the next chapter on oligopoly with entry.

The concept of Nash equilibrium is central to a situation in which information is complete (each firm knows the market demand and the cost functions of all firms) and in which firms cannot form binding agreements. A Nash equilibrium is formally defined as follows: Let n be the number of firms, A the set of all possible actions, and π_i the profit function of firm i; a^* is a Nash equilibrium if $a^* \in A$ and $\pi_i(a^*) \geq \pi_i(a_1^*, \ldots, a_{i-1}^*, a_i, a_{i+1}^*, \ldots, a_n^*)$ for all $a_i \in A$ and for $i = 1, \ldots, n$. In other words, the combination a^* of strategies is a Nash equilibrium if each a_i^* belongs to the set of feasible strategies and if, given the actions chosen by the other $n - 1$ firms, it is impossible for any one firm to increase its profits by adopting an action other than the equilibrium one. It needs to be emphasized that this concept of equilibrium requires the players to hold the view that the actions of their competitors cannot be manipulated.[7]

A Cournot equilibrium is a Nash equilibrium. For an industry composed of a given number of firms n (thus excluding entries and exits) and over only one time period, it is assumed that each firm chooses a level of production q_i, and, given the demand function of the industry, price is determined at a level at which total demand is equal to the output of the industry. Let $p = f(q)$ be the inverse demand function, where $q = \Sigma_{i=1}^{n} q_i$ denotes total output. Total costs of production differ from one firm to another and are written for firm i as

$$C_i = c_i(q_i) + F_i,$$

where $c_i(q_i)$ is variable cost and F_i is fixed cost. The profits of this firm are therefore

$$\pi_i(q_1, \ldots, q_n) = q_i f(q) - c_i(q_i) - F_i.$$

An output vector $(q_1^*, \ldots, q_n^*)$ constitutes a Cournot-Nash equilibrium[8] if each of its components q_i^* is an optimal output of firm i, knowing that other firms produce q_j^* $(j \neq i)$:

$$\pi_i(q_1^*, \ldots, q_n^*) \geq \pi_i(q_1^*, \ldots, q_{i-1}^*, q_i, q_{i+1}^*, \ldots, q_n^*)$$

$$\text{with } q_i \geq 0, \; \forall i = 1, \ldots, n.$$

For each firm the equilibrium relation between its market share and its degree of monopoly measured by the margin between price and marginal cost can then be easily established. Assuming that the π_i satisfy sufficient conditions for differentiability, the first-order conditions for maximization of profits by firm i are, for $q_i > 0$,

$$f(q) + q_i \frac{df(q)}{dq} \cdot \frac{dq}{dq_i} - c_i'(q_i) = 0. \tag{3.1}$$

According to Cournot's hypothesis, $dq/dq_i = 1$.

This implies the assumption that each firm either subjectively believes that a change in its output has no effect on the quantity its competitors wish to produce or has been convinced by its competitors that, no matter what it does, they will not change their output. An example of this second situation is one in which sellers are bound to their buyers by long-term contracts for fixed quantities of supply.

Define the Lerner index $\mathcal{L}_i$ as the margin between equilibrium price and marginal cost of firm i, and denote by ε the elasticity of demand (in absolute value) facing the industry and by $m_i = q_i^*/q^*$ the equilibrium market share of firm i. We get in this case

$$\mathcal{L}_i = \frac{p^* - c_i'}{p^*} = \frac{m_i^*}{\varepsilon^*}, \qquad i = 1, \ldots, n. \tag{3.2}$$

Relation (3.2) shows that for a noncooperative Cournot behavior the higher the market share of firm i in equilibrium, the higher its degree of monopoly ceteris paribus. But it also shows that a significant market share can correspond to a total lack of monopoly power (price equal to marginal cost) if demand elasticity tends to infinity.

In order to find a relation between monopoly power and degree of concentration, we need to aggregate the individual Lerner indexes. Then the problem mentioned in section 3.1 arises again; a value judgment must be made to determine how the individual indexes are to be aggregated. Let us assume, for instance, that we want to compare two industries, each characterized by a situation of duopoly. The individual Lerner indexes in the first industry are 0.4 and 0, respectively, whereas in the second they are 0.2 and 0.2. A priori, the first industry could be considered to manifest a greater degree of monopoly because of the greater margin held by the first firm; the second industry could be judged, however, to be in a worse situation because all firms have some monopoly power; and finally both industries could be placed on the same footing, because on average they have the same excess margin of prices. Among the various possible weights, a plausible choice is the market share of each firm:

$$\mathcal{L}(\mathcal{L}_1, \ldots, \mathcal{L}_n) = \sum_{i=1}^{n} m_i \mathcal{L}_i.$$

By using this arithmetic mean of individual degrees of monopoly weighted by respective market shares, we can see that the equilibrium relation (3.2) implies

$$\mathcal{L} = \frac{\sum_{i=1}^{n} m_i^2}{\varepsilon} = \frac{H}{\varepsilon}, \tag{3.3}$$

where H is Herfindhal's measure of industrial concentration. Moreover, if marginal costs are assumed to be constant, the term on the left-hand side can be written

$$\mathcal{L} = \frac{pq - \sum_{i=1}^{n} c_i' q_i}{pq} = \frac{\pi + F}{R},$$

which corresponds to the industry's gross profit to revenue ratio.[9] This implies that, for an industrial configuration in noncooperative equilibrium, the industry's profits are an increasing function of concentration and a decreasing function of elasticity of demand.[10]

Four useful remarks on this result are worth noting. First, the choice of Herfindhal's index is not at all necessary. Contrary to what many authors have asserted (see, for example, Curry and George (1983) and the references cited there) and as shown by Encaoua and Jacquemin (1980), it would be incorrect to conclude from the equilibrium relation (3.3) that there is sufficient justification for the measure H, as it is positively correlated with Lerner's aggregate index. In fact, all depends on the weighting system adopted. For example, by using the geometric mean of the individual Lerner indexes for each firm, we would obtain an equilibrium relation at the industry level between the aggregate measure and the entropy measure of concentration:

$$\mathcal{L} = \prod_i \mathcal{L}_i^{m_i} = \prod_i m_i^{m_i}/\varepsilon = \frac{e^{C_E}}{\varepsilon}, \tag{3.4}$$

where

$$C_E = \sum_{i=1}^{n} m_i \ln mi$$

and e is the base of the natural logarithm. Once again, the choice of a particular measure of concentration is a subjective one. For instance, when in calculating the degree of concentration the user wishes to attach a lower weight to the largest firms, believing those to be more likely to achieve economies of scale, the measure C_E might prove to be preferable.

A second remark is that under the conditions of this model, in particular the existence of positive fixed costs, there is no reason to believe that the Cournot equilibrium converges to a competitive equilibrium when the number of firms increases without limit. This convergence is only possible in special cases, for example, when entry is free or when the optimal scale is sufficiently small compared to total demand (Novshek 1980, 1984). Walrasian equilibrium then turns out to be a limiting case of a Cournot regime with entry in such a way that "price-taking" behavior is explained rather than assumed. For example, with the "heroic" hypothesis that all firms have the same constant average cost, implying $m_i = 1/n$, expression (3.3) becomes

$$\frac{p - c'}{p} = \frac{1}{\varepsilon n} \tag{3.3'}$$

such that for $n \to \infty$, price tends to be restored to the level of marginal (and average) cost. But conversely, if it is assumed that the technology of firms is not convex, the average cost curve being U-shaped, the presence of an increasing number of firms must correspond to an increase in prices, allowing a recovery of the increased costs. For large n the Cournot outcome does not approximate the competitive situation, and larger n may decrease welfare by leading to less competitive market prices. In fact, if it is accepted that equilibrium profits must be greater than or equal to zero, a positive fixed cost implies an upper limit to the possible value of n.

More generally, some theoretical work in this area, (for example, Roberts (1980)) has shown that for "large" finite economies, there can be Cournot-Nash equilibria that are nowhere near the competitive equilibria for these economies. I return to this question in chapter 4, which is devoted to entry phenomena.

A third remark is that a Cournot equilibrium rests on the hypothesis that all firms make the same conjecture, which is that, following a modification in their own output, there will be no change in the output of their competitors. One way of widening the range of possible conjectures is to rewrite the term dq/dq_i, which appears in equation (3.1), in the form

$$dq/dq_i = 1 + \sum_{j \neq i} \frac{dq_j}{dq_i} = 1 + \alpha_i,$$

where the term α_i is the conjectural variation suggested by Bowley (1924) and Frisch (1951).

The conjectural variation can be viewed as a subjective probability related to the reactions that firm i expects from other firms in the neighborhood of a certain optimum.[11] It may also be interpreted as a conjecture "imposed" on firm i by other firms as a result of credible threats they have made. Moreover, an interpretation in terms of elasticity is obtained by aggregating expression (3.1) over n firms and choosing the market share of firm i as the weight for each $\mathcal{L}_i$:

$$\mathcal{L} = \sum_{i=1}^{n} m_i \mathcal{L}_i = \frac{1}{\varepsilon} \sum_{i=1}^{n} m_i m_i \frac{dq}{dq_i}. \tag{3.5}$$

The expression

$$\frac{dq}{dq_i} m_i = \frac{dq}{dq_i} \frac{q_i}{q}$$

is the elasticity conjectured by firm i of the total output of the industry with respect to changes in its own output. For an industry of homogeneous goods, price depends only on total quantity q such that this elasticity measures the degree of influence that firm i believes it can exert on the price. In a monopoly this elasticity takes the value of 1; if firms are price takers, it is equal to 0; and if Cournot's hypothesis is satisfied, it comes back to the market share.

Alternatively, expression (3.5) can be written so as to bring out the roles of concentration and degree of collusion in the equilibrium relation involving the industry's rate of margin. Given

$$\frac{dq}{dq_i} = 1 + \sum_{j \neq i}^{n} \frac{dq_j}{dq_i} = 1 + \alpha_i, \quad \forall i = 1, \ldots, n,$$

we have

$$\mathcal{L} = \frac{1}{\varepsilon} \sum_{i=1}^{n} m_i(m_i + m_i\alpha_i) = \frac{H}{\varepsilon}(1 + \alpha).$$

The term $\alpha \equiv \Sigma_{i=1}^{n} \alpha_i q_i^2 / \Sigma_{i=1}^{n} q_i^2$ is the firm's mean conjectural variation (Cowling and Waterson 1976). Note that its maximum value is $(1/H) - 1$, corresponding to monopoly equilibrium, and its lowest value is 0, corresponding to Cournot's noncooperative equilibrium.

Define $\beta \equiv H\alpha/(1 - H)$, which in a way expresses the degree of collusion. We then have

$$\mathcal{L} = \frac{H}{\varepsilon} + \frac{\beta(1 - H)}{\varepsilon} = \beta \frac{1}{\varepsilon} + (1 - \beta)\frac{H}{\varepsilon}, \quad (3.6)$$

given that $\beta \in [0, 1]$, because $\alpha \in [0, (1/H) - 1]$.

Industry's rate of profit margin corresponds to a convex combination of $1/\varepsilon$ and H/ε, with weight given by β.

When there is total collusion ($\beta = 1$), joint profits are maximized and the equilibrium solution is a monopoly: $\mathcal{L} = 1/\varepsilon$. At the other extreme, when the degree of collusion is at its minimum, corresponding to Cournot's noncooperative equilibrium ($\beta = 0$), we go back to expression (3.3).

A final point to note is that, given a particular weighting

system, expression (3.6) suggests a dissociation of the roles of adopted behavior and degree of concentration. This dissociation should not, however, make us lose sight of an important aspect brought out by the equilibrium relations, namely, the *endogenous nature of the degree of concentration*.

To illustrate this better, let us adopt a particular hypothesis on the value of dq_j/dq_i (in this sense, see Dixit and Stern (1982)). Let $dq_j/dq_i = \gamma \, (q_j/q_i)$ for $j \neq i$. An increase of 1% in q_i is assumed to provoke an increase of $\gamma\%$ in the output of each of the other firms. The coefficient γ applies therefore to the ratio of market shares of firms i and j. The equilibrium relation (3.1) is then rewritten as[12]

$$p + q_i f'(q)\left[1 + \gamma \sum_{j \neq i}^{n} (q_j/q_i)\right] - c_i' = 0, \tag{3.7}$$

given that

$$\sum_{j \neq i} dq_j/dq_i = \gamma \sum_{j \neq i} q_j/q_i.$$

Expression (3.7) can also be written

$$p(1 - [\gamma + (1 - \gamma)m_i]/\varepsilon) = c_i'. \tag{3.8}$$

Assume that there are n active firms and that each has constant marginal cost. By summation, we get

$$p\left[n\left(1 - \frac{\gamma}{\varepsilon}\right) - \frac{1 - \gamma}{\varepsilon}\right] = \sum_{i=1}^{n} c_i'. \tag{3.9}$$

If the demand curve is approximated by a constant elasticity curve, say $q = A_p^{-\varepsilon}$, equation (3.9) can be solved for price. If we define $\bar{c} = \Sigma \, c_i'/n$, equation (3.9) becomes

$$p = \bar{c}\Big/\left(1 - \frac{\gamma}{\varepsilon} - \frac{1 - \gamma}{n\varepsilon}\right).$$

Once the equilibrium price is determined, the value of the market share of firm i can easily be calculated as a function

of the parameters of the problem. Dividing equation (3.8)
by equation (3.9), we get

$$m_i = \frac{\varepsilon - \gamma}{1 - \gamma} - \frac{c_i'}{\bar{c}}\left(\frac{\varepsilon - \gamma}{1 - \gamma} - \frac{1}{n}\right).$$

The endogenous market share depends not only on
technological variables but also on demand conditions and
the type of behavior assumed. All measures of concentration, that is, aggregation of the m_i, will in turn depend on
the same parameters.

In conclusion, in an industrial configuration of equilibrium, concentration and profitability are jointly determined by the exogenous variables of the system, among
which are the expectations adopted by firms concerning
their rivals. In this sense indexes of concentration are not
measures that allow the prediction of performances on the
basis of causal relationships, but rather form approximations of these performances.[13,14]

Without a theory of formation of conjectural variations, a
whole range is a priori possible, corresponding to a wide
taxonomy, and various equilibria become possible (Laitner
1980). The selection of a particular equilibrium is determined from surveys on expectations and behavior or from
econometric studies of the industry.[15] An alternative way
to choose one of the equilibria is to require that certain
theoretical conditions be satisfied.[16] One such condition is
to require that the behavior that a firm attributes to another
correspond to the behavior actually adopted by the other
firm when it maximizes its profits. Failing this, there will
be inconsistency, and revisions will be necessary. Many
authors (Bresnahan 1981, 1983; Ulph 1983) have tried to
resolve this problem (which is essentially dynamic) in a
static context. It is worth presenting their approach insofar
as it serves as a relay to intertemporal approaches. In a
duopoly the conjectural variation is a conjecture made by

firm 1 on the reaction of firm 2 to its decision; on the other hand, the reaction function determines the quantity actually produced by firm 2 for all quantities produced by firm 1. There is then "rational conjectural variation" if the conjectural variation coincides at equilibrium with the derivative of the reaction function.

Assume that there are two firms producing a homogeneous good such that $q = q_1 + q_2$; also assume constant marginal costs and linear conjectures of slope r, with $r = \alpha_1 = \alpha_2$. The profits of firm 1 are

$$\pi_1 = f(q)q_1 - cq_1 - F_1.$$

A first-order condition is

$$f(q) + q_1 \frac{df}{dq} \frac{\partial q}{\partial q_1} - c_1 = f(q) + q_1 \frac{df}{dq}(1 + \alpha) - c_1 = 0$$

(3.10)

for

$$\frac{\partial q}{\partial q_1} = 1 + \frac{dq_2}{dq_1} = 1 + \alpha.$$

Total differentiation of the implicit function (3.10) with respect to q_2 gives

$$f'(q)\frac{\partial q}{\partial q_2} + \frac{dq_1}{dq_2} f'(q)(1 + \alpha) + q_1(1 + \alpha)f''(q)\frac{\partial q}{\partial q_2} = 0.$$

(3.11)

For $dq_1/dq_2 = \rho_{21}$, expression (3.11) becomes

$$f'(q)(1 + \rho_{21}) + \rho_{21}f'(q)(1 + \alpha) + q_1(1 + \alpha)f''(q)(1 + \rho_{21})$$
$$= 0.$$

(3.12)

By rearranging terms, we get

$$\rho_{21} = \frac{dq_1}{dq_2} = - \frac{f'(q) + (1 + \alpha)q_1 f''(q)}{f'(q)(2 + \alpha) + (1 + \alpha)q_1 f''(q)}.$$

The question then is: Given the hypothesis of symmetry $\alpha_1 = \alpha_2$, under what conditions is the conjecture made by one firm regarding the behavior of the other identical with the equilibrium value of the slope of the other firm's reaction function?

In the framework of the previous model, if the assumed conjectural variation is that all change in output by one of the two firms is automatically canceled by an equivalent change in the opposite direction by the competitor, we have $\alpha_1 = \alpha_2 = -1$; we would expect quantity to remain fixed and price to be constant at the competitive equilibrium. In this case the conjecture is rational, because

$$\rho_{21} = -\frac{f'(q)}{f'(q)} = -1.$$

On the other hand, if we assume a linear demand ($f''(q) = 0$) and a Cournot-type conjecture ($\alpha_1 = \alpha_2 = 0$), then $\rho_{21} = -\frac{1}{2}$. This conjecture is not rational; each firm wrongly assumes that, for all variations in its own quantity of output, the output of the other firm remains constant.

More generally, Bresnahan (1981) has been able to establish the conditions under which the noncooperative equilibrium with conjectural variations is unique. This approach, however, is subject to many limitations. Results are established for a duopoly, conjectures are only locally rational, and conjectural variation is a constant independent of the level of output of the firm formulating the conjecture.[17] Even more disputable, a static framework is used to analyze a dynamic phenomenon: In this context of simultaneous actions, it is then almost "by chance" that a conjecture turns out to be rational. In fact the idea of reacting to decisions taken by others requires a *temporal* process such that, on the basis of observed behavior, initial conjectures can be validated or modified over time. The reactions of others will then reduce the number of possible actions and will in the end impose a consistent behavior on firms that over a certain period of time maximize their realized profits. Models have been constructed along these lines, where the choice of a quantity of output for a given period is a function of all the quantities of the previous period. A strategy therefore emerges as the choice of a decision at each moment t, depending on the history of the game at that moment. The strategy chosen by a firm will be the one that maximizes the firm's realized profits, given the strategies of the other firms. An industrial configuration corresponding to a *dynamic Cournot-Nash equilibrium* consists of a combination of n functions $\phi_1^*, \ldots, \phi_n^*$, that is, players' strategies, such that no change in one of these functions may bring about any increase in realized profits. Various authors[18] have developed similar models using techniques of dynamic programming. Apart from the difficulties related to the question of existence of this type of equilibrium, this approach unfortunately leads to another limitation, namely, the multiplicity of possible equilibria. Indeed, as with the concept of a static Nash equilibrium, the notion of a dynamic Nash equilibrium implies that from each player's point of view the strategies of the other players are taken as given and are part of the exogenous environment.[19] In a temporal framework this implies the possibility of a large number of equilibria, including some involving empty threats. Because my perspective is one of interaction between strategies and environment such that the environment is somewhat manipulated over time in order to create and perpetuate positions of power, this "naive" approach is unacceptable, and another concept of equilibrium is required. This notion is introduced and illustrated in chapter 4, which is devoted to barriers to entry. Once we have acknowledged the dynamics of oligopoly, the processes of entry and exit must be incorporated.

3.3 Oligopolies and Price Competition

It is useful to contrast models of oligopoly in which quantity is the decision variable with those in which price plays this role.

In his well-known critique of Cournot's model, Bertrand considers it more reasonable to assume that firms fix prices, not quantities. One can answer this objection partly. It is no doubt true that, if firms do not commit themselves (more or less) irrevocably to realize a fixed level of output, price should be the decision variable; but on the other hand, when quantity is (more or less) fixed in advance, either because it must be planned ex ante and storage costs are high or because it corresponds to a contractual commitment, the choice of output level is central. This reply, however, is upheld better if quantities are interpreted in terms of capacity and if the competition under study is of long term (price competition concerns the short term). The selection of a level of output then corresponds to the choice of the scale of production appropriate for realizing this level.[20]

Bertrand's model itself is not immune to criticism. It requires not only that competition be in prices but also that output be realized after demand has been allocated among firms. A strange result is then obtained: With homogeneous goods, competition between duopolists leads to an equilibrium industrial configuration in which prices and marginal costs are equal; two firms are therefore sufficient to obtain the same outcome as perfect competition and the absence of any degree of monopoly, without any necessity of a process of entry. As we shall see, this result corresponds to a discontinuity in demand. Given two firms i and j, let p_i be the price offered by firm i, $q = q(p)$ be the total demand function, and c be the unit production cost, which is identical and constant for both firms.[21] If buyers are perfectly informed on offered prices, they will go to the firm with the lowest price:

$$q_i^d(p_i, p_j) = q(p_i) \qquad \text{if } p_i < p_j.$$

If displayed prices are identical and given that goods are perfectly substitutable in the utility function of buyers, these buyers will be randomly distributed; if there are many buyers, it can be assumed that each firm will get half the market:

$$q_i^d(p_i, p_j) = q(p_i)/2 \qquad \text{if } p_i = p_j.$$

Finally, if firm i offers a price higher than that of firm j, then

$$q_i^d(p_i, p_j) = 0 \qquad \text{if } p_i > p_j.$$

In this situation and denoting by p_j the lowest price announced by the rival, firm i sells nothing at a price slightly higher than p_j but occupies the whole market at a price slightly lower than p_j. The only Nash equilibrium is then made up of the pair $(p_i^*, p_j^*) = (c, c)$. Indeed if $p_i > p_j > c$, firm i makes zero profits, whereas by applying a price $p_j - \varepsilon$, it could get the whole market with positive profits $(p_j - \varepsilon - c)q$. Furthermore, if $p_i = p_j > c$, firm i gains profits of only $(p_i - c)q(p_i)/2$; then, by simply choosing a price $p_i - \varepsilon$, firm i will increase its profits from $(p_i - c)q(p_i)/2$ to $(p_i - \varepsilon - c)q(p_i - \varepsilon)$ for a sufficiently small ε. On this basis, it can easily be shown that there is no profitable deviation from (c, c).

To go beyond this rather unrealistic result, various hypotheses of the model have been challenged. I retain one, namely, perfect symmetry among firms as well as among goods.[22] We see how, first, asymmetry in behavior and then differences in goods lead to equilibria of a different nature.

That firms differ from each other in structure, objectives,

and strategies is an essential feature of real industrial situations. Generally, relationships between firms and individuals are characterized by asymmetries rather than by symmetries that have been traditionally assumed.

Stackelberg's approach is probably one of the first to have specifically introduced asymmetry in the chronology of the game (while maintaining a static framework of analysis). One of the hypotheses he has analyzed is indeed the case in which one of the duopolists assumes the role of a price leader: Firm 1 knows the response function of its rival, who behaves as a follower; firm 1 chooses a price (to which the follower reacts) in order to optimize its objective function. The strategies of the two firms are therefore no longer the same.[23]

In the model of asymmetric oligopoly that I consider, quantity is the decision variable of a set of firms who, by choosing it, determine a selling price, knowing the global supply function of the other firms; these other firms form a "competitive fringe" producing a quantity such that their marginal cost is equal to the price. Let us examine this situation in more detail.[24]

Let K be the dominant group composed of the k largest firms of the industry, and let $(n - k)$ be the firms making up the competitive fringe. The demand function facing the industry is $q = f(p)$, and the aggregated supply function of the fringe is $q_c = \phi(p)$. The demand function facing the dominant cartel is therefore

$$q_K = q - q_c = f(p) - \phi(p).$$

If we assume that this demand function is invertible, then the profit function of one of the k firms is given by

$$\pi_i(q_1, \ldots, q_k) = p(q_k)q_i - c(q_i) - F_i,$$

where $p(q_k)$ is the inverse of the demand function. The maximization of profits by each firm of the dominant group requires that

$$p + q_i \frac{dp}{dq_k} \frac{\partial q_k}{\partial q_i} - c_i'(q_i) = 0, \qquad i = 1, \ldots, k. \qquad (3.13)$$

It can then be assumed that the k firms adopt between themselves a noncollusive Cournot behavior while perceiving the dominant role they collectively play in the determination of price: $\partial q_k / \partial q_i = 1$. Hence we have

$$p - c_i' = q_i \Big/ \left(\frac{dq}{dp} + \frac{dq_c}{dp}\right), \qquad (3.14)$$

where the absolute value of dq/dp is adopted, or

$$\mathcal{L}_i = m_i \left(\frac{1}{\varepsilon + \eta(1 - C_K)}\right), \qquad i = 1, \ldots, k, \qquad (3.15)$$

where $m_i = q_i/q$ is the market share of firm i,

$$\varepsilon = \frac{dq}{dp} \frac{p}{q}$$

is the absolute value of elasticity of demand facing the industry,

$$\eta = \frac{dq_c}{dp} \frac{p}{q_c}$$

is the (positive) elasticity of supply of the competitive fringe, and

$$C_K = \frac{\displaystyle\sum_{i=1}^{k} q_i}{q} = \sum_{i=1}^{k} m_i$$

is the degree of concentration measured by the sum of the market shares of the k dominant firms.

To obtain the equilibrium degree of monopoly within the dominant group, I add the individual degrees, weighted by the market share of each firm i in the output of the dominant group:

$$\mathcal{L} = \sum_{i=1}^{k} \frac{q_i}{q_K} \mathcal{L}_i = \sum_{i=1}^{k} \frac{m_i}{C_K} \mathcal{L}_i = \frac{H_K C_K}{\varepsilon + \eta(1 - C_K)}, \qquad (3.16)$$

where

$$H_K = \sum_{i=1}^{k} \left(\frac{m_i}{C_K}\right)^2$$

is Herfindhal's measure of concentration within the dominant group. Expression (3.16) indicates that in equilibrium the degree of monopoly within an industry is higher with a higher concentration among the k firms of the dominant group[25] and with a more significant aggregated share compared to total sales. Therefore the value of the Lerner index is positively correlated with both the asymmetry between the oligopolistic and competitive groups and the asymmetry within the dominant firms.[26] On the other hand, a high elasticity of the demand function and a high price elasticity of the supply function of the competitive fringe reduce the degree of monopoly. This elasticity of the supply function can be interpreted as a response from not only incumbent competitive firms but also potential entrants who are attracted by the increasing market price.

At this stage I need to raise an important question that will clarify the significance of the price leadership model (and of Stackelberg's model). The way in which the asymmetry of roles is introduced in the model is totally exogenous, and the reasons why some firms act as leaders and some as followers is left unexplained. Now, in general, it is more profitable to be a follower because the follower sells all quantity that it judges desirable at the same price as the leader. The leader, on the contrary, is constrained by the reaction function of the follower. This argument is akin to the remark by Schelling (1963), for whom being given the role of leader is "an unprofitable distinction evaded by the apparent follower and assumed per force by the apparent leader" (p. 23). Two questions therefore must be considered. First, is it possible to develop a theory in which the allocation of the asymmetric roles is endogenous? Second, once the stage at which firms choose their roles has been reached, is it possible to define the conditions under which this allocation of roles will be stable in the sense that no firm will be induced to change its role? Little work exists in the literature on the first aspect.[27] Boyer and Moreaux (1983b) have shown that, in a static framework and for a duopoly with a homogeneous product and a strategy space composed of prices and quantities, if technologies are sufficiently different, then there will be collusion between the duopolists: The firm having the *less* efficient technology (higher costs) will act as leader, and the firm having the *more* efficient technology (lower costs) will act as follower. This result illustrates the error of systematically labeling as "dominant" those firms having price leadership. Many authors have nevertheless adopted this point of view. For instance, Worcester (1957) writes:

The dominant firm situation is one in which the price leader has a control over the industry price and its own output, but not over rivals' output. The dominant firm behaves passively in regard to the output of small firms . . . [isolating] its own demand curve by subtracting from the industry demand curve the estimated total quantity supplied by all rivals at each price. (p. 388)

Starting from this disputable version of a dominant firm, it is easy to show the leader's automatic decline, indeed its disappearance (especially when this "dominant" firm has only price as its competitive weapon), and to therefore suggest that the long-run equilibrium is the competitive one. We will see this essential theme again in the context of dynamic analysis and the phenomenon of entry.

The second question, that of the stability of a situation of imperfect competition in which there exist one or more

economic agents playing the role of price leader has been
the subject of some research. Thus d'Aspremont et al.
(1983) have shown that there is always stability for a cartel
establishing the leading price if the set of firms is finite. To
illustrate the argument, let there be a set of n identical
firms, k of which form a cartel that fixes the price in such a
way that profits are maximized for each firm in the cartel,
given that production of competitive firms is determined
by the equality between the fixed price and their marginal
cost.[28] Because all firms sell at the same price and because
the firms in the fringe choose without any constraints the
output that maximizes their profit at this price, we have

$$\pi_f(k) \geq \pi_l(k),$$

where $\pi_f(k)$ and $\pi_l(k)$ denote the profits of the firms in the
fringe and in the cartel, respectively.

Two types of stability are then defined. A cartel made up
of k members has internal stability if $k \geq 1$ and if $\pi_f(n, k - 1) \leq \pi_l(n, k)$. It has external stability if $k \leq n - 1$ and if $\pi_l(n, k + 1) \leq \pi_f(n, k)$.[29] The cartel is called stable if there is
internal and external stability at the same time. Disregard-
ing cases of equal profits, d'Aspremont et al. then wrote a
simple algorithm showing that there is always a stable cartel. Having established that the profits of each firm in the
cartel increase with the size of the cartel, d'Aspremont et
al. assumed that the cartel with $k = 0$ has external stability,
whereas the cartel with $k = 1$ has internal stability. If the
case $k = 1$ also has external stability, then a stable cartel
has been found. Otherwise, the case $k = 2$ is considered;
this has internal stability, or else the process would have
stopped at $k = 1$. If $k = 2$ has external stability, the search
for a stable cartel has ended. According to the algorithm,
either a stable cartel is found with $k < n$, or the algorithm
reaches $k = n$. In this case, $k = n$ has internal stability,

Table 3.1
Maximum profit for five firms for different cartel sizes[a]

Profit	Number of firms in cartel (k)					
	0	1	2	3	4	5
π_l	–	0.126	0.130	0.137	0.149	0.161
π_f	0.125	0.128	0.136	0.151	0.177	–

a. $n = 5$; $D(n, p) = 5(1 - p)$.

and, because all the firms are included, the monopoly cartel is stable.

An example illustrates the theorem. Table 3.1 is constructed for an industry composed of five firms, each of
which has the cost function $c(q) = \frac{1}{2}q^2$, with the demand
function $D = n(1 - p)$. The table indicates for the possible
different sizes of the cartel the maximum profit of each firm
in equilibrium.

The unique stable cartel is the one composed of three
firms; it has internal stability, because $\pi_l = 0.137 > \pi_f =$
0.136, and external stability, because $\pi_f = 0.151 > \pi_l =$
0.149. The crucial point is that a firm tempted to enter the
cartel or to leave it should not compare its actual profits
with those of a firm that is in the other position. For example, in order to decide whether or not to leave the cartel,
a firm that is a member of the cartel should not compare its
profits of 0.137 with those gained by a member of the
fringe group, that is, 0.151. Indeed, if the firm leaves the
cartel, it would modify in some way the market structure
in the sense that it would change the industrial configuration, increasing the size of the fringe group and decreasing that of the cartel. This would lead to a change in price
such that the profit gained in the new situation by joining
the fringe group (0.136) is below the actual profits the firm
received as a member of the cartel (0.137).

A lesson to be drawn from this illustration is that, in situations in which firms take into account the interactions between their decisions and their environmental conditions, an equilibrium of the leader-follower type can be stable without any tendency of the leader(s) to disappear.[30]

Another kind of asymmetry is the one affecting the *products* of firms within a given industry. These products are not generally considered as the same by consumers: It is the whole phenomenon of imperfect substitutability arising from product differentiation or different localities.[31] It is customary to assume that the practice of product differentiation itself is based on the production of either distinct varieties of the same basic good (horizontal differentiation) or goods of different quality (vertical differentiation).[32] The first type of differentiation is similar to spatial differentiation in the sense that small differences among the varieties of a good of a given quality are treated as differences of location of sellers, who are themselves constrained by transport costs. In Hotelling's tradition, competition between firms is considered here to be "localized": Each mark or variety competes only with a reduced number of direct rivals, even if the number of sellers in the global market is large; the real degree of concentration is much higher than a measure based on the whole of the market would suggest, and the likelihood of collusion (see, for instance, Archibald et al. (1986))[33] is itself higher.

The analysis of the second type of differentiation has developed on the basis of the contribution by Lancaster (1979), who considers that the quality of a good changes when the absolute value of most of its "characteristics" increases or decreases per unit of the good.

This aspect of the theory of oligopoly opens the door to a wide variety of "nonprice" policies that pose many problems. A first aspect is the relation between price and nonprice policies. From the firm's viewpoint these policies can be related either by complementarity or by substitutability, the absence of interaction being unlikely. Among the many contributions in the literature, I mention the study by Feichtinger (1982), who in the framework of a model of optimal control used a state variable (the market share) and two control variables (price and advertising). Combining the models of Phelps and Winter and of Jacquemin, Feichtinger discussed the saddle point property of the equilibrium and showed that optimal policies of price and advertising follow a contradictory behavior; thus a continuously increasing price level should be accompanied by a decreasing level of publicity, avoiding contradictory effects on the state variable. A second aspect concerns welfare, which has also been the subject of many studies. None of these unequivocally establishes a hypothesis favorable to some socially optimal level of nonprice policies. A simple illustration is the case of a monopolist trying to extract a surplus from the introduction of a new product. The total surplus (TS; consumer + producer) induced by such an introduction is

$$TS = \int_0^{q_m} f(q)dq,$$

where q_m is the equilibrium output produced by the monopolist and $f(q)$ is the demand function. For a constant elasticity of demand ε the total revenue (TR) obtained by the firm can be written

$$TR = \int_0^{q_m} MR(q)dq = \left(1 - \frac{1}{\varepsilon}\right) \int_0^{q_m} f(q)dq = TS\left(1 - \frac{1}{\varepsilon}\right),$$

where MR is the marginal revenue. The less elastic demand is, the smaller the proportion of total surplus that the monopolist can capture. This suggests situations in which the firm will not introduce products that are socially worthwhile because it is unable to appropriate enough surplus.

While referring to the literature for other refinements, I must emphasize that with the recent models of product differentiation, the number of different varieties of a particular product and the number of products of different qualities are no longer initial conditions; they result from the choices of producers who aim to partition the set of consumers and to extract the consumer surplus of each segment. Just as for the degree of concentration (see section 3.2), the diversity and the quality of goods become endogenous. In these situations the long-run market equilibrium may correspond to the case in which the number of firms is small. Thus, in contrast to an approach such as Hart's (1979), the works of Lane (1980), Gabszewicz and Thisse (1980), and Shaked and Sutton (1983) show that, for an industry differentiated and characterized by a continuum of possible goods, either in the space of characteristics or in the geographic space, there are situations in which the industry can allow only a Nash equilibrium with a limited number of firms and situations in which supranormal profits are possible. This is particularly the case when there is little diversity among consumers (in terms of either tastes or incomes). The idea is that in the absence of major differences suppliers lose only a little of the consumer surplus by offering only the best quality product at a price that allows even the poorest consumer to purchase. On the contrary, if incomes (or tastes) vary substantially, it is in the suppliers' interest to segment the market in order to exploit the differences in surplus among consumers, which in turn allows a larger number of firms to be present. The label of "natural oligopoly" applied by Shaked and Sutton to this kind of configuration obviously has a completely different significance from the same label applied to "perfectly contestable" markets; in the first case, features of demand play a crucial role, whereas in the second, technology is the determining factor.

Once again, these developments require explicit consideration of the phenomenon of entry in a dynamic context, which is the subject of the next chapter.

3.4 Biological Games and Strategies

Before analyzing equilibrium models of dynamic competition, it is useful to look briefly at recent studies in biology that go beyond the simple mechanisms (mentioned in chapter 2) that were supposed to ensure the selection of the fittest. These studies resort to concepts of equilibrium close to the ones used in theories of imperfect competition, the best known being the notion of a stable strategy in the context of evolution (evolutionary stable strategy, or ESS). This can be presented as follows. Consider a homogeneous population in which meetings between the members of a pair take place at random. In this case the contests are said to be symmetric, and each agent will behave identically in all contests. A strategy is the specification of an individual's behavior in a contest.

Let v and μ be the strategies of two players that meet, and let S be the set of all strategies. The expected gain or utility when playing v against μ is $E(v, \mu)$. Smith (1974) defined a stable strategy as a strategy satisfying one of the following two conditions:

1. $E(v, v) > E(\mu, v)$ for $\mu \neq v$, $\mu \in S$.

2. If $E(v, v) = E(\mu, v)$ for some μ, then $E(v, \mu) > E(\mu, \mu)$.

If a player is confronted with an opponent coming from a population whose members play strategy v, the condition

$$E(v, v) \geqslant E(\mu, v), \qquad \forall \mu \in S,$$

would correspond to a Nash equilibrium. In fact, we saw in section 3.2 that a set of actions forms a Nash equilibrium if the action of each player is the preferable one for that player, given the actions of the other players; in this case, a player has no reason to use a strategy other than v. Let me stress that a player in Nash equilibrium considers the actions of others as given, a hypothesis that may be less open to criticism in the context of biological games than in industrial organization.

The contribution of the biologist J. Maynard Smith is mainly the second condition, which allows the reduction of the number of Nash equilibria by requiring stability. When the strict inequality of the first condition is not satisfied and when a better second response to v exists, other than v itself, namely, the strategy μ, then the strategy v must itself be a response to μ, which is better than μ.

Besides the relation between two players, the notion of an ESS is used to describe the equilibrium of a large population in which all individuals adopt the same strategy v to start with. If a mutant appears within this population, using some strategy μ instead of v, the mutant will tend to be eliminated if Smith's second condition is satisfied, so long as such a mutant has a low relative frequency. The equilibrium strategy v is called stable in this sense. A simple example illustrates this approach. Assume a situation in which the two meeting players, who come from the same homogeneous population, can adopt two types of behavior: either a peaceful attitude or an aggressive one. The non–zero sum game, in normal form, is represented by a matrix of gains. The strategies of player I are the rows of the matrix, and those of player II are the columns. Each element of the matrix represents an outcome of the game, made up of two numbers, the first being the gain of the first player and the second that of the other.

I	II Peaceful	Aggressive
Peaceful	(2,2)	(0, 10)
Aggressive	(10, 0)	$(-5, -5)$

If a player adopts an aggressive behavior and is confronted with another player who decides to adopt a peaceful strategy, the first player has a gain of 10, whereas the pacifist has a gain of zero. On the other hand, if there is a meeting between two individuals adopting a belligerent behavior, each will lose 5. A meeting between two pacifists brings a gain of 2 to each. There are two Nash equilibria for the two (pure) strategies retained in the table, corresponding to (0, 10) and (10, 0). Indeed, if the initial position corresponds to one of these pairs, it is in no player's interest to change strategy, given that of the other. If another kind of strategy is introduced, namely, a mixed strategy, there is a third equilibrium. In this case the players attach probabilities to their behavior; they adopt a mixture of pure strategies in proportions they choose. In my example the corresponding equilibrium is attained when each player chooses the peaceful strategy with probability $5/13$ and the aggressive strategy with probability $8/13$. Indeed, given the mixed strategy of player I (resp. player II), the choice of strategies of player II (resp. player I) always leads to the same outcome such that there is no advantage in changing strategies. For instance, suppose that player II knows the random choice of player I, based on an allocation of $5/13$ peaceful, $8/13$ aggressive. If player II chooses the aggressive behavior, the expected gain will be

$$\frac{5}{13}(10) + \frac{8}{13}(-5) = \frac{10}{13},$$

and if player II chooses the peaceful behavior, the expected gain will be

$$\frac{5}{13}(2) + \frac{8}{13}(0) = \frac{10}{13}.$$

A priori, the interpretation of an equilibrium of mixed strategies, in the framework of a static model in which decisions are made only once, is not clear, but it has a great interest in the evolutionist perspective. Indeed, assume successive random meetings between two players coming from a homogeneous population. This being the case, the two equilibria corresponding to pure strategies cannot constitute ESS equilibria because they require pairs of complementary behavior, aggressive and peaceful. On the other hand, the only point of symmetric ESS equilibrium in which the players use the same strategy is our mixed strategy equilibrium; any other mixed strategy is rejected as it would yield less gain.[34] We can interpret the mixed strategy equilibrium as a situation in which the probabilities attached to each type of behavior are the equilibrium values of the proportion of the population (of infinite size) having, respectively, peaceful and aggressive behavior. Any other distribution of the population would not be an ESS equilibrium, in the sense that the proportion of individuals adopting the pure strategy corresponding to the lower expected gain would tend to decrease until equality is established between the expected gains of the two strategies.

In this interpretation the state of equilibrium requires the coexistence of different behaviors; contrary to the views expressed in chapter 2, selection does not lead to the elimination of one type to the benefit of another, because each offers an advantage if it is not too generalized within the population. This state of equilibrium corresponds to what is referred to as a "stable polymorphism."[35]

Many other aspects, such as replacement of the hypothesis of a homogeneous population by an analysis of asymmetries[36] that correlate with performance (different sizes, occupation of a privileged location, or incomplete information), introduction of a larger set of strategies, and recognition of problems of bluff and credible threats[37] multiply the number of possible equilibria in an impressive manner.

Beyond this, conditions favorable to the existence of cooperative behavior and its persistence in the course of evolution can be studied. Axelrod (1984) has analyzed in the ecological context the emergence and subsistence of a system of "live and let live" within living species. He has shown through simulation the prevalent superiority of simple rules of behavior over sophisticated optimizing strategies. One of the longer lasting rules is the one called Tit for Tat, in which one starts by adopting a cooperative behavior and then does what the rival has done in the previous round. He has also shown that cooperation can emerge even without foresight.

All these studies question the existence of a unique criterion and a unique mechanism of selection in social interactions. Forms of competition are varied, and adjustment processes are far from always being univocal, that is, associating only one type of outcome with each environment. Furthermore, stable equilibria can be characterized by the coexistence of behavior of different types, corresponding to a real polymorphism. Hence an a priori guarantee that a unique form will prevail or that a specific optimum will emerge from evolutionary forces at work is unlikely.

Notes

1. See in particular Houssiaux (1958), Perroux (1964), Bienayme (1971), Jenny and Weber (1976), and Jacquemin and de Jong (1977).

2. For an analysis of these properties, see Hannah and Kay (1977) and Encaoua and Jacquemin (1980). One of the first studies was carried out by Hildenbrand and Paschen (1964).

3. Note that the index of concentration (and the equivalent number) tends to n as θ tends to zero. Herfindhal's index can be rewritten in a way to distinguish the two characteristics that a measure of concentration ought to reflect, namely, the number of firms in the market being considered and the degree of inequality of the distribution of their relative shares. Given that the variance of market shares is defined as

$$\sigma^2 = \frac{\Sigma\, m_i^2}{n} - \frac{1}{n^2} = \frac{H}{n} - \frac{1}{n^2},$$

Herfindhal's index can in fact be written

$$H = n\sigma^2 + \frac{1}{n}.$$

4. The general entropy of order θ according to Renyi (1970) is

$$G_\theta = \frac{1}{1 - \theta} \ln \sum_{i=1}^{n} m_i^\theta.$$

5. If m_i is defined as the probability that a random variable Z takes the value z_i, then E represents in information theory the amount of uncertainty associated with the value of Z and, equivalently, the mean value of information received when the value of Z is observed or the mean value of "surprise" when one is informed of the value of Z. For a uniform probability distribution, uncertainty and surprise are at a maximum.

6. For an application of this formula to the decomposition of concentration in European enterprises, see Jacquemin and Kumps (1971). Jacquemin (1975) also suggested using an equivalent formula to decompose the global degree of diversification into a narrow diversification (close to the basic production) and a wide diversification. This approach has been applied to the 500 largest American enterprises by Jacquemin and Berry (1979).

7. According to Moulin (1981, p. 58), two opposing hypotheses can be used so that the players do not take into account the influence they could exert on other players; either there exists an obstacle to all communication among players in such a way that each player, unaware of the interests of others, is only guided by self-interest or there is a total lack of trust, making it impossible to make either promises leading to coalitions of interest or threats that would be considered credible.

8. For the Cournot equilibrium to be a fixed point, it is assumed that the profit function is quasi-concave, which ensures the continuity of reaction functions. If this hypothesis is not satisfied, either because of the demand function or because of nonconvexity of the cost function, the existence of an equilibrium can still be obtained, particularly if the firms are small relative to the size of the market. See, in particular, Bamon and Fraysse (1984).

9. If there are economies of scale, the ratio of profits to turnover is equal to the Lerner index plus a term measuring the profit imputable to the difference between marginal and average costs in equilibrium. This term is positive for decreasing productivity.

10. The resulting expression, $(pq - \Sigma_{i=1}^{n} c_i'q_i)/pq = H/\varepsilon$, can also be used to express the link between consumer surplus (CS) and concentration. Expressing CS as a function of price, we can write

$$CS = F(p) = F\left(\frac{\sum_{i=1}^{n} c_i'q_i/q}{1 - H/\varepsilon}\right), \quad \text{with } F' < 0.$$

For a given average cost level, a higher H corresponds to a higher price-cost margin and a lower consumer surplus.

11. The hypothesis implying $\alpha_i = -1$ may be interpreted as expressing the will to maintain a stable (competitive) price: The firm expects that any attempt to change market price by a modification of its output will be canceled by an equivalent modification in the opposite direction by its competitors.

12. This hypothesis poses the problem of an interior solution if $\gamma = 1$. In this case expression (3.7) cannot hold for all i when the c_i are not equal. If all firms try to maintain their market share ($dq_j/dq_i = q_j/q_i$), only those having the lowest costs will survive.

13. For a general discussion, see Donsimoni et al. (1985).

14. It must be emphasized that various authors have shown the role of the degree of concentration for product differentiation (Encaoua and Jacquemin 1978; Schmalensee 1982), for vertical integration (Waterson 1980), and for diversification in various markets (Clarke and Davies 1983; Encaoua et al. 1986).

15. For such studies, see Iwata (1974) and Appelbaum (1979).

16. Among these conditions can be mentioned the one in which empty threats are excluded from the strategies. This last aspect will be examined in chapter 4.

17. Boyer and Moreaux (1983a) showed that, if each duopolist's conjectural variations are also a function of the output level of its competitor, almost all situations in which each duopolist has non-negative profits may lead to an equilibrium with rational conjectural variations. Hence there is no reduction in the number of equilibria.

18. See, in particular, Cyert and de Groot (1970), Friedman (1977, ch. 5), and Kalai and Stanford (1983).

19. The formal definition of a dynamic Nash equilibrium is as follows (Tirole 1983): Let $A_{it}(H_t)$ be the decision set of player i at time t, where H_t is the history of the game at that time. A strategy $s_i = (s_{it}(H_t))$ is the choice of an action in $A_{it}(H_t)$ for each t and each H_t at this time. A set of strategies $(s_1^*, \ldots, s_n^*)$ is a dynamic Nash equilibrium if and only if for each i,

$$\pi_i\,[a(s_i^*,\, s_{-i}^*)] \geqslant \pi_i[a(s_i,\, s_{-i}^*)]$$

for any other feasible strategy s_i, given that $a(s)$ denotes the series of actions generated by the set of strategies s.

20. Kreps and Scheinkman (1983) developed a model of two time periods in which the duopolists simultaneously and independently choose a capacity during the first period and enter into price competition in the second, under capacity constraints set up in period 1. They showed that under certain hypotheses about demand the unique configuration of equilibrium is that of Cournot. One way of interpreting this two-stage game is to consider it as a mechanism that eliminates the mythological "auctioneer" required to determine price in the Cournot model. Note that this approach is close to that of Edgeworth, who, in going beyond Bertrand's model, introduced capacity constraints linked to the fact that capital cost prevents excessive initial accumulation. See also Shubik (1980).

21. It is well known that, when marginal costs are increasing, the Bertrand model does not have an equilibrium in pure strategies. One solution is then to resort to mixed strategies. For a model of this type, see Allen and Hellwig (1986), who showed that, independently of the number of firms, there is always a positive probability that some firms will apply a price close to monopoly price.

22. In Cournot's model there is asymmetry in cost functions corresponding to different market shares.

23. Let the "leading" firm 1 pronounce price p_1, and let firm 2 react, according to Cournot, by choosing $p_2 = \phi_2(p_1)$. Firm 1 maximizes $\pi_1[p_1, \phi_2(p_1)]$ with respect to p_1, and the first-order condition is $\pi_1^1 + \pi_1^2 \phi_2' = 0$. If a time lag is introduced, firm 2 uses $p_{2t} = \phi_2(p_{1,t-1})$, and firm 1 maximizes

$$\sum_{t=1} r_1^{t-1} \pi_1[p_{1,t}, \phi_2(p_{1,t-1})],$$

where r_1 is the rate of discount.

24. This analysis is based on Encaoua and Jacquemin (1980).

25. Assuming that the dominant group acts as a cartel, we have

$$\mathcal{L} = \frac{C_k^2}{\varepsilon + \eta(1 - C_K)}$$

with $\partial\mathcal{L}/\partial C_k > 0$.

26. Let us note that, because a positive margin between price and marginal cost exists only for the leading group, although the monopoly power of the members of the competitive fringe is null by construction, we cannot obtain a relation for the whole industry. Given that

$$\sum_{i=1}^{k} \left(\frac{m_i}{C_K}\right)^2 = \frac{\sum_{i=1}^{k} m_i^2}{(C_K)^2},$$

it is obviously possible to replace H_k with $\bar{H}/C_k^2$ in expression (3.16), where $H = \Sigma_{i=1}^k m_i^2$ is a truncated Herfindahl index. Hence we could have

$$\mathcal{L} = \frac{\bar{H}}{C_K[\varepsilon + \eta(1 - C_K)]}. \tag{3.16'}$$

In this case the sign of $\partial\mathcal{L}/\partial C_K$ is not obvious.

27. At the conceptual level, Moulin (1981) studied games in normal form with two players in Stackelberg equilibria by identifying situations in which the players are fighting to go first (it is in the interest of each of the two players to take leadership) and situations in which they are fighting to go second (each player wants to play second to force the other player to reveal its choice of strategy first). The game is called a rational Stackelberg game if the strategies adopted by the two players give both of them a higher profit than they would gain from any other pair of strategies. See also chapter 4.

28. Extensions to this model have been put forward by Donsimoni (1985) and Rothschild (1984).

29. By convention, the null cartel, $k = 0$, has internal stability, and the monopoly, $k = n$, has external stability.

30. D'Aspremont et al. (1983) showed that, on the contrary, when there is no indivisibility in the size of firms, a continuum of agents (therefore an infinitesimal influence from each of them) excludes stability.

31. A general presentation is given by Phlips (1984).

32. For cars there is horizontal differentiation if a given model (say, a Renault 4) is offered with different varieties (or options), whereas there is vertical differentiation when different models are offered (say, a Renault 4 and a Renault 20). This example suggests that the distinction is in fact a matter of degree.

33. Asymmetry, characteristic of Hotelling-type approaches, contrasts with the hypothesis of symmetry adopted in models of monopolistic competition. These models assume a representative buyer who buys all the different makes such that each firm affects (and is affected by) all the others in a symmetric way. See, for example, Dixit and Stiglitz (1977).

34. Selten (1983) provides a general argument. Let us assume that within a large population using the same mixed strategy v of equilibrium, a mutant appears who resorts to another strategy μ. This mutant has a low frequency, $\varepsilon > 0$. In this slightly disturbed situation an adversary in a conflict will play v with a probability $1 - \varepsilon$ and the strategy μ of the mutant with probability ε. The mutant will be eliminated if the following inequality is satisfied:

$$E(v, (1 - \varepsilon)v + \varepsilon\mu) > E(\mu, (1 - \varepsilon)v + \varepsilon\mu),$$

that is, if resorting to strategy v yields more than using strategy μ. Because this inequality is bilinear, we can also write

$$(1 - \varepsilon)E(v, v) + \varepsilon E(v, \mu) > (1 - \varepsilon)E(\mu, v) + \varepsilon E(\mu, \mu).$$

This inequality is satisfied for all μ and for all sufficiently small ε only if (v, v) is an equilibrium. If this were not the case, we would have $E(v, v) < E(\mu, v)$, μ being a better response, in such a way that for sufficiently small ε the inequality would be reversed. Let us assume that (v, v) is indeed an equilibrium. Two situations can then arise: Either μ is not a better alternative response to v (in this case, the second inequality is satisfied for sufficiently small values of ε, given that $E(v, v) > E(\mu, v)$), or μ is a better alternative response to v, in which case the first terms on both sides of the second inequality are equal. The inequality is then satisfied if and only if $E(v, \mu) > E(\mu, \mu)$, which corresponds to Smith's second condition. Let me stress that Riley (1979) showed that a stable strategy as defined by Smith is less appropriate if we deal with a finite population.

35. If many examples of this kind exist in nature, various analogies present themselves equally in economics, be it a decision on a price war or of entry into a market. Cornell and Roll (1981) have for their part applied the concept of ESS equilibrium to the stock market and to rules of promotion within an organization.

36. For studies on this theme in theoretical biology, see Selten (1980), Parker (1983), and Hammerstein and Parker (1982). The last article presents an analysis of a version of the falcons-doves model with incomplete information. In such a model, in which animals adopt different roles, such as that of a proprietor or an invader in a territorial conflict, and in which the winner is the one prepared to resist the longer ("war of attrition"), an ESS strategy could give the status of winner to the one who has the least to lose or the least ability to fight. This result, which depends on certain conditions being satisfied (for instance, an irreversible commitment to complete a "round" after having decided to participate in a fight) is paradoxical in relation to a selection process that works, in principle, in favor of the one having the most to gain or the least to pay for persisting.

37. The possibility that animals have to bluff or lie in their intra- and interspecific relations has been the subject of many studies. In his rebuttal to the criticisms of Moynihan (1982), Smith (1982)

responds that if an animal can win a competition without risks by simply indicating its intention to attack, nothing will prevent it from giving this signal, whether or not it is true. In situations of competition, such signals relative to intentions are not considered totally trustworthy. On the other hand, communication regarding the scale of resources actually retained would become more credible with increasing cost of the retention of (or increase in) these resources. In chapter 4 we see that a similar argument has been developed on the strategic behavior of firms.

References

M. Adelman. 1969. "Comments on the H concentration measure as a number equivalent." *Review of Economics and Statistics* 51:99–101.

B. Allen and M. Hellwig. 1986. "Bertrand-Edgeworth oligopoly in large markets." *Review of Economic Studies* (forthcoming).

E. Appelbaum. 1979. "Testing price taking behaviour." *Journal of Econometrics* 9 (3):283–294.

G. Archibald, B. Eaton, and R. Lipsey. 1986. "Address models of value theory," in *New Developments in the Analysis of Market Structure*, J. Stiglitz and F. Mathewson (eds.). London: Macmillan, 3–47.

C. d'Aspremont, J. Gabszewicz, and J. Thisse. 1979. "On Hotelling's stability in competition." *Econometrica* 47(5):1145–1150.

C. d'Aspremont, A. Jacquemin, and J. F. Mertens. 1986. "A measure of aggregate power in organizations." *Journal of Economic Theory* (forthcoming).

C. d'Aspremont, A. Jacquemin, J. Gabszewicz, and J. Weymark. 1983. "On the stability of dominant cartels." *Canadian Journal of Economics* 16:17–25.

R. Axelrod. 1984. *The Evolution of Cooperation.* New York: Basic Books.

R. Bamon and J. Fraysse. 1984. "Existence of Cournot equilibrium in large markets." Cahier 8311, Université de Toulouse. Also to be published in *Econometrica*.

A. Bienayme. 1971. *La croissance des entreprises* (The growth of firms). Paris: Bordas.

A. Bowley. 1924. *The Mathematical Groundwork of Economics*. Oxford: Clarendon Press.

M. Boyer and M. Moreaux. 1983a. "Conjectures, rationality, and duopoly theory." *International Journal of Industrial Organization* 1:23–41.

M. Boyer and M. Moreaux. 1983b. "Distribution des rôles et espaces de strategies dans la théorie du duopole de Stackelberg" (Distribution of roles and the space of strategies in Stackelberg's theory of duopoly). Cahier 8318, Universite des Sciences Sociales de Toulouse.

T. Bresnahan. 1981. "Duopoly models with consistent conjectures." *American Economic Review* 5:934–945.

T. Bresnahan. 1983. "Existence of consistent conjectures: Reply." *American Economic Review* 5:457–470.

R. Clarke and S. Davies. 1983. "Aggregate concentration, market concentration and diversification." *Economic Journal* 1:182–192.

B. Cornell and R. Roll. 1981. "Strategies for pairwise competitions in markets and organizations." *Bell Journal of Economics*, spring, 201–213.

K. Cowling and M. Waterson. 1976. "Price-cost margins and market structure." *Economica* 43:267–274.

B. Curry and K. George. 1983. "Industrial concentration: A survey." *Journal of Industrial Economics* 31(3): 203–255.

R. Cyert and M. de Groot. 1970. "Multiperiod decision models with alternating choice as a solution to the duopoly problem." *Quarterly Journal of Economics* 84(3):410–429.

H. Demsetz. 1974. "Two systems of belief about monopoly," in *Industrial Concentration: The New Learning*, D. Goldschmid, H. Mann, and J. Weston (eds.). Boston: Little, Brown, 164–184.

A. Dixit and N. Stern. 1982. "Oligopoly and welfare: A unified presentation with application to trade and development." *European Economic Review* 19:123–143.

A. Dixit and J. Stiglitz. 1977. "Monopolistic competition and optimum product diversity." *American Economic Review* 67(3):297–308.

M. P. Donsimoni. 1985. "Stable heterogeneous cartels." *International Journal of Industrial Organization* 4:451–467.

M. P. Donsimoni, P. Geroski, and A. Jacquemin. 1985. "Concentration indices and market power: Two views." *Journal of Industrial Economics* 33:419–434.

D. Encaoua and A. Jacquemin. 1980. "Degree of monopoly, indices of concentration, and threat of entry." *International Economic Review* 21(1):87–105.

D. Encaoua, A. Jacquemin, and M. Moreaux. 1986. "Global market power and diversification." *Economic Journal* 96:525–533.

G. Feichtinger. 1982. "Saddle point analysis in a price advertising model." *Journal of Economic Dynamics and Control* 4:319–340.

J. Friedman. 1977. *Oligopoly and the Theory of Games*. Amsterdam: North-Holland.

J. Friedman. 1983. *Oligopoly Theory*. Cambridge: Cambridge University Press.

R. Frisch. 1951. "Monopoly and polypoly: The concept of force in economy." *International Economic Papers* 1:10–20.

J. Gabszewicz and J. Thisse. 1980. "Entry (and exit) in a differentiated industry." *Journal of Economic Theory* 22:327–338.

P. Geroski. 1983. "Some reflections on the theory and application of concentration indices." *International Journal of Industrial Organization* 1:79–94.

P. Hammerstein and G. Parker. 1982. "The asymmetric war of attrition." *Journal of Theoretical Biology* 96(4):647–682.

L. Hannah and J. Kay. 1977. *Concentration in Modern Industry*. London: Macmillan.

O. Hart. 1979. "Monopolistic competition in a large economy with differentiated commodities." *Review of Economic Studies* 46:1–30.

P. Hart. 1975. "Moment distribution in economics: An exposition." *Journal of the Royal Statistical Society*, ser. A, part 3, 138:423–434.

W. Hildenbrand and H. Paschen. 1964. "Ein axiomatish begrün-
detes Konzentrationsmass" (A measure of concentration with an
axiomatic basis). *Eurostat* 3:53–61.

J. Hirshleifer. 1982. "Evolutionary models in economics and law:
Cooperation versus conflict strategies," in *Research in Law and
Economics*, R. Zerbe (ed.). London: JAI Press, vol. 4, 1–60.

J. Houssiaux. 1958. *Le pouvoir de monopole* (Monopoly power).
Paris: Sirey.

G. Iwata. 1974. "Measurement of conjectural variations in
oligopoly." *Econometrica* 42:947–966.

A. Jacquemin. 1975. "Une mesure entropique de la diversification" (An entropy measure of diversification). *Revue Economique*
5:834–838.

A. Jacquemin and C. Berry. 1979. "Diversification and corporate
growth: An entropy measure." *Journal of Industrial Economics*
27:359–369.

A. Jacquemin and H. de Jong. 1977. *European Industrial Organization*. London: Macmillan.

A. Jacquemin and A. M. Kumps. 1971. "Changes in the size
structure of the largest European firms: An entropy measure."
Journal of Industrial Economics 20:36–42.

F. Jenny and A. P. Weber. 1976. *L'entreprise et les politiques de
concurrence* (The firm and policies of competition). Paris: Editions
d'Organisation.

E. Kalai and W. Stanford. 1983. "Conjectural variation strategies
in dynamic Cournot games." Discussion paper 575, Northwest-
ern University.

D. Kreps and J. Scheinkman. 1983. "Quantity precommitment
and Bertrand competition yield Cournot outcomes." *Bell Journal of
Economics* 14(2):326–337.

J. Laitner. 1980. "Rational duopoly equilibria." *Quarterly Journal of
Economics* 95(4):641–662.

K. Lancaster. 1979. *Variety, Equity and Efficiency*. New York: Columbia University Press.

W. Lane. 1980. "Product differentiation in a market with en-dogenous sequential entry." *Bell Journal of Economics* 11(1):237–260.

A. Mas-Colell. 1983. "Walrasian equilibria as limits of non-cooperative equilibria I." *Journal of Economic Theory* 30(1):153–170.

H. Moulin. 1981. *Théorie des jeux pour l'économie et la politique* (Game theory for economics and politics). Paris: Hermann.

M. Moynihan. 1982. "Why is lying about intentions rare during some kinds of contests?" *Journal of Theoretical Biology* 97:7–12.

W. Novshek. 1980. "Cournot equilibrium with free entry." *Review of Economic Studies* 47:473–486.

W. Novshek. 1984. "Perfectly competitive markets as the limits of Cournot markets." *Journal of Economic Theory* 35:78–82.

Y. Ono. 1982. "Price leadership: A theoretical analysis." *Economica* 49:11–20.

G. Parker. 1983. "Arms races in evolution: An ESS to the opponent-independent costs game." *Journal of Theoretical Biology* 101:619–648.

F. Perroux. 1964. *L'économie du XXéme siécle* (The economy of the 20th century). Paris: PUF.

L. Phlips. 1984. *The Economics of Price Discrimination*. London: Cambridge University Press.

A. Renyi. 1970. *Probability Theory*. Amsterdam: North-Holland.

J. Riley. 1979. "Evolutionary equilibrium strategies." *Journal of Theoretical Biology* 76:109–123.

K. Roberts. 1980. "The limit point of monopolistic competition." *Journal of Economic Theory* 22:256–278.

R. Rothschild. 1984. "Market price and the stability of cartels." *Economic Letters* 15:127–131.

T. Schelling. 1963. *The Strategy of Conflict*. Cambridge: Harvard University Press.

R. Schmalensee. 1982. "The new industrial organization and the economic analysis of modern markets," in *Advances in Economic*

Theory, W. Hildenbrand (ed.). Cambridge: Cambridge University Press, 253–285.

R. Selten. 1980. "A note on evolutionary stable strategies in asymmetric animal conflicts." *Journal of Theoretical Biology* 84:93–101.

R. Selten. 1983. "Evolutionary stability in extensive 2-person games." Working paper 121, Universität Bielefeld.

A. Shaked and J. Sutton. 1983. "Natural oligopolies." *Econometrica* 51(5):1469–1483.

C. Shannon. 1948. "A mathematical theory of communication." *Bell System Technical Journal* 27:379–423, 623–656.

M. Shubik. 1980. *Market Structure and Behaviour*. Cambridge: Harvard University Press.

J. Maynard Smith. 1974. "The theory of games and the evolution of animal conflicts." *Journal of Theoretical Biology* 47:209–221.

J. Maynard Smith. 1978. "The evolution of behavior." *Scientific American* 239:18, 176–178.

J. Maynard Smith. 1982. "Do animals convey information about their intentions?" *Journal of Theoretical Biology* 97:1–5.

G. Stigler. 1950. "Monopoly and oligopoly by merger." *American Economic Review* 40:23–24.

H. Thiel. 1967. *Economics and Information Theory*. Amsterdam: North-Holland.

J. Tirole. 1983. "Jeux dynamiques: un guide de l'utilisateur" (Dynamic games: A user's guide). *Revue d'Economie Politique* 93(4):551–575.

D. Ulph. 1983. "Rational conjectures in the theory of oligopoly." *International Journal of Industrial Organization* 2:131–154.

M. Waterson. 1980. "Price-cost margins and successive market power." *Quarterly Journal of Economics* 1:135–150.

D. Worcester. 1957. "Why dominant firms decline." *Journal of Political Economy* 65:338–346.

4

Barriers to Entry: Natural and Constructed

In the previous chapters two aspects of the new industrial organization have been contrasted. On the one hand, some authors present a view of the industrial world in which the symmetry of economic agents predominates. This symmetry is either postulated from the outset or presented through Darwinian analogies as the ultimate outcome of a selection process that ultimately eliminates the deviants. In the long run only efficient agents survive, and market equilibrium is optimal. On the contrary, other researchers insist that models of imperfect competition, which also have their counterparts in biology, give rise to industry configurations in which a small number of asymmetric firms gaining nonzero profits coexist at equilibrium.

A crucial criterion distinguishing these different studies relies on the conditions of entry in the market. In section 4.1 I show, in the framework of contestable markets examined in section 2.2, how the virtues of free entry discipline markets, even if there is asymmetry between incumbent firms and entrants and even if production is characterized by economies of scale. In section 4.2 I first review the principal asymmetries that constitute the barriers to entry and that are related to the concept of sunk costs and then present models incorporating these aspects. In the third section I am concerned with firms' strategies aimed at manipulating their rivals' environment by creating or developing asymmetries susceptible to forming new barriers to entry; illustrative models will clarify the conditions of credibility and profitability of such investments. I present in section 4.4 the major strategic weapons at firms' disposal in situations of both perfect and incomplete information. Finally, in section 4.5 I discuss the limitations of strategic rationality.

4.1 Free Entry and Competitive Equilibrium

Freedom of entry and exit in an industry is one of the essential driving forces of competition. The selection of the most efficient firms and the realization of competitive equilibrium in a dynamic setting rest on this basis. In the last few years many studies have shown that this phenomenon plays a disciplinary role, even when it appears to be failing. Two aspects are presented: the decline over time of the "dominant firm" and the contested role of economies of scale as a barrier to entry.

The first aspect is the evolution of a "dominant" firm confronting a fringe of small price-taking firms. Gaskins's model (1971) has influenced this point greatly. For one firm leading in price and for an entry rate linearly related to the current price of the industry and given the absence of economies of scale and cost advantages in favor of the dominant firm, Gaskins showed that price decreases with entry and that the stationary state is characterized by a competitive situation. Let $x(t)$ be the level of sales at time t of the competitive fringe, and let $dx(t)/dt = \dot{x}(t)$ be the rate of entry. For a limit price p_L, an average cost c, and a reaction coefficient k, all assumed constant, the rate of entry is directly proportional to the difference between current price $p(t)$ and p_L, that is,

$$\dot{x}(t) = k(p(t) - p_L).$$

The limit price p_L is defined as the maximum price that can be charged without attracting any entry. The difference between p_L and the average cost of the dominant firm measures the possible barrier from which the firm benefits. For a demand $f(p(t))$ facing the industry, the dominant firm maximizes[1]

$$V = \int_0^\infty e^{-rt}(p(t) - c)(f(p(t)) - x(t))dt$$

such that the value (not discounted) of the corresponding Hamiltonian is written

$$H = (p(t) - c)[f(p(t)) - x(t)] + \lambda(t)k(p(t) - p_L),$$

where the dual variable $\lambda(t)$ is the implicit price attached by the firm to an additional entry of a competitor at each moment of time. According to the maximum principle, the necessary conditions for price policy to be optimal are

$$\partial H/\partial p = (p - c)f'(p) + [f(p) - x] + \lambda k = 0, \qquad (4.1)$$

$$\dot{\lambda} = \lambda - \frac{\partial H}{\partial x} = \lambda + (p(t) - c), \qquad (4.2)$$

$$\dot{x} = k(p - p_L), \qquad x(0) = x_0. \qquad (4.3)$$

Condition (4.1) can be written

$$-\lambda k = f'(p)(p - c) + f(p) - x, \qquad (4.4)$$

where $\lambda(t)$, the implicit price of an additional entry, is negative; that is, $\lambda(t)$ corresponds to a cost. The condition for a "myopic," or static, maximization of profits, where λ is zero, is

$$\partial \pi/\partial p = f'(p_m)(p_m - c) + f(p_m) - x = 0, \qquad (4.5)$$

where p_m is the monopoly price. For the zero value of expression (4.5) to be compatible with the positive value of expression (4.4), we must have $p^* < p_m$: Optimal price level should at every moment t along the optimal path be below the price that maximizes short-term profits. Hence, by incorporating the process of entry in the dynamics of the model, the price policy that would have been followed in the absence of this phenomenon is indeed tempered.

It is then possible to determine the market share of the dominant firm, $m = [f(p) - x]/f(p)$, in stationary equilibrium.

By using equations (4.1) and (4.2), we can eliminate the auxiliary variable because equation (4.4) implies

$$\lambda(t) = \frac{x - f(p) - (p - c)f'(p)}{k}.$$

We get

$$\dot{x} = k(p - p_L), \tag{4.6}$$

$$\dot{p} = \frac{k(p_L - c) + x - f(p) - (p - c)f'(p)}{-2f'(p) - (p - c)f''(p)}. \tag{4.7}$$

The optimal price policy will lead to a long-term market share of

$$\hat{m} = \frac{f(p_L) - \hat{x}}{f(p_L)},$$

where $\hat{x}$ is the sales level of the competitive fringe at the stationary point. To obtain the value of $\hat{x}$, we must set equations (4.6) and (4.7) equal to zero and solve simultaneously:

$$\hat{x} = (p_L - c)f'(p_L) + f(p_L) - k(p_L - c).$$

Using this value for $\hat{x}$, we can rewrite the market share of the dominant firm in stationary equilibrium:

$$\hat{m} = \frac{k(p_L - c) - f'(p_L)(p_L - c)}{f(p_L)}.$$

Hence it is clear that, in the absence of cost advantages in favor of the "dominant" firm, the only equilibrium limit price is the price that is equal to average (and marginal) cost: $p_L = c$. It follows that the dominant firm must disappear ($\hat{m} = 0$), and the industry's total output is realized by the entire set of identical firms constituting the competitive fringe at an industry price equal to marginal cost.[2]

This happy outcome is by no means unexpected. Indeed it is hard to see how a firm having only price as its competitive weapon, not enjoying any cost advantage, acting in a context of total certainty, and not benefiting from any kind of delay in its rivals' response could maintain any kind of asymmetric position over a long period. The dominance of the leading firm here, as in the corresponding static model (see section 3.3), is illusory, and its disappearance is only the elimination of the firm that was already the weakest.

A second situation in which entry could play its disciplinary role, even when it appeared to be failing, is in economies of scale. Whether in a static or a dynamic context, the existence of important economies of scale has been considered a "natural" barrier to entry (Scherer 1980) that reduces the long-run equilibrium configuration to a small number of price-making firms.

Various authors,[3] however, have recently shown that these are not genuine barriers because the technological conditions of production affected both incumbents and entrants in the same way. To understand the argument, two points need to be stressed. On the one hand, fixed costs are independent of the scale of production and are not reduced, even over a long period, by a decrease in output: They can be eliminated only over a long period by total cessation of activity. On the other hand, the capital for which economies of scale exist is a priori available for alternative usage.

For example, in the domain of air transport between different localities, there are economies of scale over a given period in the sense that larger cargo require bigger carriers, ensuring a lower cost per unit of cargo. But it is possible a priori for an airline company to enter a new market (a new line) temporarily and without cost while fully exploiting economies of scale by employing its transport equipment in other lines the rest of the time. More generally, in the domain of perishable goods (such as services), where output must be offered at the time of demand, a firm may simultaneously exploit economies of scale and engage in a process of rapid and costless entry and exit. This kind of argument allows Baumol et al. (1982) to assert that in such situations fixed costs do not constitute a barrier to entry and that incumbents cannot make profits in equilibrium, even if they benefit from economies of scale. Figure 4.1 illustrates the difference between this argument and the traditional outlook on monopolistic

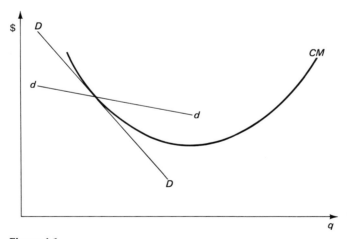

Figure 4.1
Chamberlin's equilibrium and contestable market.

competition. The demand curve *DD* rests on the potential entrant's hypothesis that incumbent firms will react to all price changes by the entrant by changing their own price in the same way. Chamberlin's equilibrium is obtained when the curve *DD* is tangent to the average cost curve. But, so long as the incumbent firms cannot change their prices instantaneously (whereas consumers respond instantaneously to price differentials), the entrant would anticipate a more elastic demand curve, *dd*, based on the hypothesis that prices applied by incumbents are fixed. Thus there is no reason why an entrant having access to the same technology (the same product) would not enter at a lower price: In a contestable market the tangency solution with the curve *DD* is not an equilibrium.

I have already stressed in chapter 2 (section 2.2), the strong conditions required for the theory of perfectly contestable markets to be applicable. I return to this question in the next section.

4.2 Barriers to Entry and Cost Asymmetry

According to Stigler (1968):

A barrier to entry may be defined as a cost of producing (at some or every rate of output) which must be borne by firms which seek to enter an industry but is not borne by firms already in the industry. (p. 67)

This conception is in line with the notion of "sunk costs," that is, costs that cannot be eliminated, even if activity is stopped completely. Once incurred, sunk costs are not part of the costs of the firm's alternative because they cannot be put to alternative use. Sunk costs create an important asymmetry between the incumbent firm and the entrant; indeed this fraction of investment is no longer part of the expenses of the incumbent firm, whereas the entrant must count it as an outlay. The entrant knows, therefore, that the scrap value of such an investment will be zero or in any case below the initial cost (net of depreciation) and must be certain that the expected revenue will be sufficient to compensate for the risk of losing this irreversible fraction of investment. Examples of such costs are innumerable. They include those costs required to establish the reputation of an entrant, including advertising expenditure for the product, as well as costs incurred in acquiring a specific technology and "know-how."[4]

Many well-known characteristics of capital (material or other) give rise to sunk costs. Some such favorable factors are a high degree of irreversibility, important specificity at the level of the product, technology, and the firm, and long durability.

One can then ask if in many situations economies of scale and sunk costs are in fact not intimately linked. Indeed the necessity to bear major fixed costs when setting up large units of production corresponds to specific, partially irreversible investments of long duration that generally have low resale value. This was recognized by Sylos-Labini (1957) when he was highlighting technological rigidities, discontinuities, and specificities related to the launch (or closure) of units of production required for large-scale operations. In this context fixed costs are indeed barriers to entry constraining the possibility of rapid entries and exits in the form of "raids." More formally, one can maintain that in the absence of sunk costs the role of economies of scale becomes doubtful, as the firm can always operate at the minimum average cost. Consider figure 4.2, in which q is the level of output, k is the rate of production per unit of time, and T measures the time horizon, such that $q = kT$. If k can be changed without any cost (absence of sunk costs), then the firm can always operate at q^*, the minimum of average costs.[5]

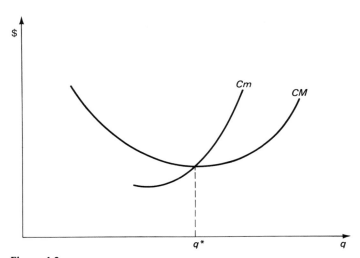

Figure 4.2
Efficient equilibrium in the absence of sunk costs.

Be that as it may, the existence of differential sunk costs allows incumbent firms to stop entry while realizing a gain at equilibrium, if we accept Sylos-Labini's postulate that incumbent firms maintain their output level whether or not entry takes place. This is shown in figure 4.3.

The incumbent firm can prevent all entry by giving up the application of its monopoly price p_M and by adopting a "limit price" p_L equal to the entrant's average and marginal cost. (Of course, if the barrier to entry is such that the entrant's average cost is equal to the monopolist's price, entry is totally blocked and the monopolist can exploit its position with impunity.)

Nevertheless there is no guarantee that this policy will be more profitable than the policy of exploiting monopoly power and allowing entrants to penetrate: The real tradeoff is between a policy of large short-run profits with a small long-term market share at one extreme and a policy of

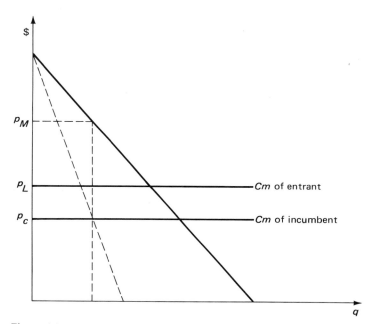

Figure 4.3
Barrier to entry and limit pricing.

limited short-run profits with a more important long-run market share on the other.

Gaskins's model, in which the same notion of limit price appears, has shown that, in fact, for an initial market share higher than the share corresponding to the stationary equilibrium, the pricing policy of the leading firm along the optimal path results in a price below the monopolist's; this price decreases as entrants appear and asymptotically approaches the limit price. Without any cost advantages the leading firm would disappear in the long run; however, as soon as the leading firm's strategy space is widened and it has other competitive weapons besides price that are liable to create cost (and/or demand) asymmetries in its favor, such a leader is likely to ascertain a truly dominant position and survive over a long period. Various models demonstrate this, including those of Jacquemin (1971), Jacquemin and Thisse (1972), Kamien and Schwartz (1975), Lee (1975), de Bondt (1977), Bourguignon and Sethi (1981), and Encaoua and Jacquemin (1980). In the last model, which is a generalization of Gaskins's model, it is assumed that the leading firm or group of k firms use besides a price policy a policy of fixed and irreversible expenses, bringing a dissuasive effect to bear on entrants. Such expenses corresponding to advertising investment, cost of research and development, or any other capital expenditure tend to increase capital costs for entrants and thus reduce entry. The rate of entry is

$$\dot{x}(t) = R(p(t), s(t)) \quad \text{with} \quad \partial R/\partial p > 0 \text{ and } \partial R/\partial s < 0,$$

where $s(t)$ is the level of fixed expenditure at time t at which potential rivals are dissuaded from entering the market after t and R is the rate of entry. The leading group maximizes

$$V = \int_0^\infty e^{-rt}[(p(t) - c)(f(p(t)) - x(t) - s(t))]dt$$

such that the value (not discounted) of the corresponding Hamiltonian is

$$H = (p - c)[f(p) - x] - s + \gamma R(p, s),$$

where the dual variable γ is the implicit cost borne by the leading firm as a result of an additional entry in the industry. The necessary conditions for policies of price and fixed expenditures to be optimal are

$$\frac{\partial H}{\partial p} = (p - c)\frac{dq}{dp} + f(p) - x + \gamma\frac{\partial R}{\partial p} = 0, \qquad (4.8)$$

$$\frac{\partial H}{\partial s} = -1 + \gamma \frac{\partial R}{\partial s} = 0,$$
(4.9)

$$\dot{\gamma} = \gamma + (p - c).$$
(4.10)

Equation (4.9) expresses the value of the implicit cost of entry:

$$\gamma = 1 \Big/ \frac{\partial R}{\partial s} < 0, \quad \text{given that } \frac{\partial R}{\partial s} < 0.$$
(4.11)

Equation (4.8) on the other hand can be rewritten

$$\mathcal{L} = \frac{p - c}{p} = \frac{1}{\varepsilon} \left[C_k + \frac{\gamma}{x} \frac{\partial R}{\partial p} (1 - C_k) \right],$$
(4.12)

where ε is the absolute value of the elasticity of demand facing the industry and $C_k = (f(p) - x)/f(p)$ is the leading group's market share at time t along the optimal path. Relation (4.12) is the dynamic counterpart of the equilibrium relation derived in the static case between the degree of monopoly measured by Lerner's index and the degree of concentration measured by the market share of the k dominant firms. Given that $\gamma < 0$, this relation shows that the degree of monopoly is lower in a dynamic situation in which entry is possible than in the static case ($\gamma = 0$). The interpretation of relation (4.12) becomes more interesting when some terms are replaced by dynamic elasticities with the following definitions:

$$\eta(t) = \frac{\partial R}{\partial p} \frac{p}{R}$$

is the elasticity of the rate of entry with respect to price policy, with $\eta(t) > 0$; and

$$\theta(t) = -\frac{\partial R}{\partial s} \frac{s}{R}$$

is the elasticity of the rate of entry with respect to expenditure policy $s(t)$, with $\theta(t) > 0$. Replacing $\gamma(t)$ by its value given by equation (4.11), we get

$$\mathcal{L} = \frac{p - c}{p} = \frac{1}{\varepsilon} \left(C_k - \frac{\eta}{\theta} \frac{s}{pq} \right). \tag{4.13}$$

Given demand elasticity and concentration, the degree of monopoly increases with decreasing price elasticity of the rate of entry ($\eta(t)$) and increasing elasticity with respect to dissuasive expenditures ($\theta(t)$). On the other hand, the ratio of fixed expenditures to the industry's turnover has a negative effect on the rate of margin. It can then be shown that at the solution of stationary equilibrium the dominant group can retain a positive market share.[6]

Yet this type of approach suffers from many limitations, the most important being that entrants do not make explicit decisions. The decision to enter or not is determined by an ad hoc rule without any assurance that the underlying behavior is optimal. Therefore we cannot talk about a Nash equilibrium. Such a formalization may be a defendable approximation for numerous anonymous candidates for entry (for example, in a situation of an influx of imports), but its weakness becomes crucial in the hypothesis of a confrontation with a small number of entrants who could possibly be important existing firms that are trying to diversify. In such situations incumbent firms and the candidates for entry are rational players who calculate their respective chances, compare forces, engage in a complex game of strategic relations, and take into account only the credible threats of their rivals. It is truly at this level that the richness of the interactions between economic agents and their environment arises.

These players, endowed with different powers, are capable not only of exploiting their initial asymmetries but

also of developing them in order to create conditions for
future actions to constrain their adversaries and limit their
freedom of choice. In order to deal rigorously with such an
outlook, new concepts and tools of analysis are required.[7]

4.3 Strategic Creation of Barriers to Entry

The strategic creation of barriers to entry rests on two requirements. First, a firm embarking on such a policy must
ensure its credibility in the eyes of its rivals in a way that
effectively constrains their behavior. Second, the firm must
be certain of its profitability in the sense that the expenditure caused by this policy is more than offset by the additional revenue resulting from it.

In his seminal book, Schelling (1960) defined a strategic
move as "one that influences the other person's choice in a
manner favourable to oneself by affecting the other person's expectations of how oneself will behave" (p. 160).
Therefore, to modify the expectations of rivals in a credible
way, what is required is an irrevocable engagement if information is complete or, if information is incomplete, an
engagement perceived as being irrevocable. Indeed the essence of credible retortion strategies resides in the volun-
tary and irreversible sacrifice of a part of one's freedom of
choice. "These are based on the paradox that the power to
constrain one's adversary depends on the power to constrain oneself irrevocably" (Schelling 1960, p. 22). No one
can tie others up if he is not tied up himself or if he does
not appear to be tied up.

A simple example illustrates this situation. Consider an
industry with no entry costs but with temporal asymmetry.[8] Firm 1 is established and must choose a level of
capital K_1 corresponding to a specific and irreversible investment (hence its costs are well sunk). Firm 2 is the entrant and chooses its capital level K_2 (having the same

characteristics as K_1) after having inquired about the level of K_1.[9] The profit functions for firms 1 and 2 are written

$$\pi_1(K_1, K_2) = K_1(1 - K_1 - K_2),$$
$$\pi_2(K_1, K_2) = K_2(1 - K_1 - K_2).$$

I assume that price competition and profit functions are reduced forms. The quadratic form of π expresses that a firm's marginal profit decreases with its own level of capital as well as with that of its rival. Firm 1 will then maximize its profit by taking into account the effect of its choice of K_1 on the choice of K_2. The maximization of profits by firm 2 requires

$$\pi_2' = 1 - K_1 - 2K_2 = 0$$

such that

$$K_2 = R_2(K_1) = \frac{1 - K_1}{2},$$

where R_2 is the reaction function of firm 2. Hence firm 1 maximizes

$$\pi_1 = K_1\left[1 - K_1 - \left(\frac{1 - K_1}{2}\right)\right].$$

In a Stackelberg equilibrium in which both firms are in the industry, we get

$$K_1 = \frac{1}{2}, \qquad K_2 = \frac{1}{4}, \qquad \pi_1 = \frac{1}{8}, \qquad \pi_2 = \frac{1}{16}.$$

Let us compare this solution with that obtained for a Cournot-Nash equilibrium in which decisions are simultaneous. By solving simultaneously the system of equations

$$\pi_1' = 1 - 2K_1 - K_2 = 0,$$

$$\pi_2' = 1 - 2K_2 - K_1 = 0,$$

we get

$$K_1 = K_2 = \tfrac{1}{3}, \qquad \pi_1 = \pi_2 = \tfrac{1}{9}.$$

We can see, therefore, that as a result of temporal asymmetry firm 1 has been able to accumulate more capital than in simultaneous equilibrium, and this has reduced the profitability of the marginal investment of firm 2, who has been constrained to reduce its level of capital. This leads to higher profits for firm 1.[10]

These results are shown in figure 4.4, which uses reaction lines and isoprofit curves. CN corresponds to the Cournot-Nash equilibrium, S to the Stackelberg-Nash equilibrium, and M to the monopoly equilibrium. Let us now assume that there exists a fixed sunk entry cost $F < \tfrac{1}{16}$.

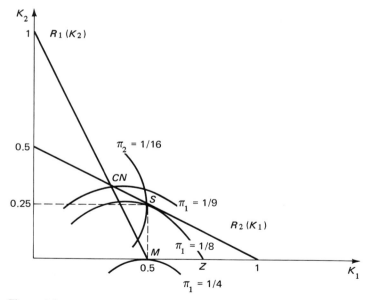

Figure 4.4
Alternative equilibria in an entry game.

In this case it is profitable for firm 1 to prevent entry, in the sense that the decrease in π_1 resulting from the increase in K_1 necessary to make entry by firm 2 nonprofitable is more than compensated for by the increase in π_1 resulting from the absence of a second firm in the industry. To determine the level of K_1 that blocks entry, we need to find only the amount of capital for firm 1 that will cancel the profits of firm 2, given the reaction function of firm 2, $K_2 = (1 - K_1)/2$:

$$\pi_2(K_2, K_1) = K_2(1 - \overline{K}_1 - K_2) - F$$
$$= \frac{1 - \overline{K}_1}{2}\left(1 - \overline{K}_1 - \frac{1 - \overline{K}_1}{2}\right) - F = 0.$$

This level is equal to

$$K_1 = 1 - 2\sqrt{F}.$$

By choosing a level of capital (between $\frac{1}{2}$ and Z in figure 4.4), firm 1 realizes profits higher than it would in a Stackelberg equilibrium:[11]

$$\pi_1 = (1 - 2\sqrt{F})(1 - 1 + 2\sqrt{F}) = 2\sqrt{F}(1 - 2\sqrt{F}) > \frac{1}{8}.$$

An extension of this type of situation to the dynamic case was carried out by Flaherty (1980b). She assumed that each firm must bear an adjustment cost in order to modify its production rate, introducing an imperfect reversibility of this rate. The incumbent can then "bind" itself, with the view to prevent entry, by adopting a high rate of production before entry. The entrant therefore knows that in case of entry the incumbent's output level can decrease only gradually because of its adjustment costs. This is indeed a credible threat from the incumbent. The entrant will deduce that during this slow decline in production its profits will be below the level corresponding to the stationary equilibrium.

These models rest on a new concept of equilibrium put forward by Selten (1975), namely, *perfect equilibrium*.[12] It must be recalled that in a dynamic Nash equilibrium (see section 3.2) firms consider all possible actions of their rivals as given, no matter what these actions may be. In contrast, a perfect equilibrium excludes possible actions corresponding to empty threats, given others' strategies: Such threats are actions that would not be put into effect if players had the occasion to execute them because such a step would work against their own interest. In other words, in a game of many time periods it is assumed that all players play in their best interests in each time period. Hence the perfect equilibrium is the only dynamic Nash equilibrium having the following property: Players' strategies for any subgame constitutes a Nash equilibrium in which each player adopts the best possible response to the strategies of other players, whether or not the possibility represented by one of the stages of the subgame actually appears on the equilibrium path. An illustration in the form of a sequential game is useful in order to capture the scope of this concept.

Consider two firms with a finite horizon in an environment of certainty. One is established in the market. I consider two situations: one in which only "innocent" behavior is allowed, in the sense that the firm does not try to influence the expectations of its potential rival, and one in which "strategic" behavior is allowed, that is, a strategy of credible threat can be deployed. The tree of the corresponding game is presented in figure 4.5.[13]

Assume first that the incumbent firm is limited to innocent behavior (upper branch of figure 4.5). If the potential entrant decides to stay out of the market, the incumbent gains a monopoly profit of π_m. If entry takes place, the incumbent can choose between "economic warfare" with a profit of π_g for the duopolists and a sharing of the market with a profit of π_d. We can assume that $\pi_m > \pi_d > 0 > \pi_g$,

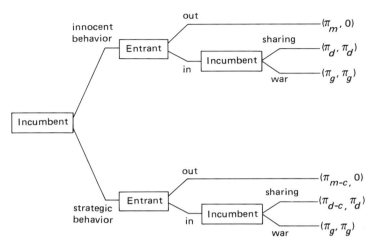

Figure 4.5
Entry game in an extensive form.

that is, duopoly is profitable but less so than monopoly, whereas war is mutually destructive. The pair of behaviors ("war in case of entry" for the incumbent and "staying out of the market" for the potential entrant) constitutes a Nash equilibrium. If we consider, however, the subgame beginning at the second node of the incumbent branch, it is clear that war is not a credible threat because it would not be the optimal response of the incumbent in case of entry, and the entrant is aware of this. This response is therefore eliminated in the context of a perfect equilibrium. On the contrary, sharing is the incumbent's optimal response because $\pi_d > 0 > \pi_g$. By reasoning by backward induction,[14] the entrant's best strategy is therefore to decide to enter the market. The pair (π_d, π_d) is the unique perfect Nash equilibrium.

It is interesting to mention here one well-known problem of repeated games. If the game of the incumbent and the entrant were played several times in a sequential process, we would expect the incumbent to be more tempted to prevent a sequence of entries, given that the dissuasive effect is exerted over many periods: Losses resulting from war during the first period could be compensated by the present value of the net gains of the resulting monopoly of following periods.[15] But when the horizon is finite, the incumbent would not adopt this aggressive behavior in the last period because this would not be in its short-run interest, and in any case the possibility of further entry does not exist. The potential entrant at this final stage is aware of this situation and will therefore decide to enter. The previous stage thus becomes the last stage, and the same reasoning applies to this stage. By forward induction it must be concluded that, in the presence of a deadline for the game, entry will never be prevented. To avoid the paradox, one of two options can be followed: either assume an infinite horizon[16] or abandon the hypothesis of complete information.

Let us return now to the second branch of the tree of the game (figure 4.5), that is, the situation in which the incumbent may have a strategic advantage linked to its capacity to retain the initiative in the market it already occupies. Assume that the incumbent has a specific and irrevocable investment corresponding to a fixed cost c providing the means to engage in war. This expenditure does not affect its profits if war actually takes place because π_g includes such an expenditure, but in the other circumstances it burdens profits. The following three stages of recursive reasoning then apply: It is credible that the incumbent firm will engage in war if its losses in case of sharing are higher than in case of war, that is, if $\pi_g > \pi_d - c$. If this is so, the entrant's optimal strategy is to stay out of the market. The incumbent, aware of this, must therefore assess recursively if its optimal behavior is to adopt innocent behavior or strategic behavior. The incumbent will opt for strategic behavior only if the corresponding final profit is higher than the profit it would gain from innocent behavior, that is, if $\pi_m - c > \pi_d$. It follows that the incumbent will use its credible threat and will prevent entry if and only if there exists a strategic commitment with a cost satisfying the condition $\pi_m - \pi_d > c > \pi_d - \pi_g$, that is, if the difference between profits of monopoly and profits of duopoly is higher than the cost of the strategic action and if the cost of the strategic action is itself higher than the difference between profits of duopoly and profits of war.

At this stage, it is useful to review briefly the principal instruments or capital expenditures liable to confer strategic advantages.

4.4 Strategic Weapons, Entry, Exit, and Mobility

Throughout the previous expositions I have tried to show that barriers to entry are far from being either inexistent or natural and that they are created partly by various types of strategic moves, that is, actions that are available to a firm in order to influence its rivals' choices by circumscribing those choices in a manner that favors the incumbent. Thus I come back to the idea that market structure and the economic environment must not be perceived as purely exogenous but, on the contrary, are partially open to manipulation by the economic agents themselves. Market power is then characterized by the capacity of a firm to modify market conditions in its own favor over time. Let me identify the major types of investment that are liable to have such an effect.

One way of classifying investments is to distinguish those that affect demand from those that influence costs.[17] On the *demand* side, the role of advertising and promotion, although often emphasized, is arguable because it has a high rate of depreciation. Nevertheless marketing allows "buying of time" until other instruments are ready for defending the market position. Moreover, with uncertainty advertising and other intangible investments create a notoriety capital and a reputation likely to influence the expectations of potential rivals. Policies of differentiation, changes of style, and imposition of one's own norms (linked to compatibility of products and equipment) are also means of increasing the fixed sunk part of cost. As to the proliferation of new products, brands, and patents by a firm, they allow preemption, that is, an extensive occupation of the geographic or characteristic space in such a way that it is no longer profitable for the entrant to respond to the remaining demand. As we saw in chapter 3, the existence of specific fixed costs associated with a locality or of high costs of mobility of fixed capital induces irrecoverable expenses and increases the profitability of the established firm vis-à-vis the entrant. The higher the sunk proportion of fixed costs, the more credible the commitments of the incumbent.

On the *cost* side the creation of excess capacity is one of the tools most analyzed. The formation of excess capacity implies a specific cost for the firm and allows the firm, in case of entry, to increase its output without its cost rising too rapidly. The role of the learning process has also been widely discussed. By adopting a low price initially, the incumbent stimulates a rapid expansion of demand for its product and hence places itself in the lower part of its learning curves, even before the entrant has had a chance to begin to compete. Clearly, learning is characterized by sunk costs because a firm cannot recoup the expenditure it has incurred by acquiring (past) production experience. There exists equally a whole series of strategies (including vertical integration and long-term contracts) vis-à-vis factor markets, be it labor, debt, and equity capital or components of a final product. These strategies can be used to create a cost differential that favors the incumbents, either by decreasing their costs or by increasing the costs of their potential rivals.

The question, then, is to determine whether the cost supplement that incumbents incur to create this differential is more than compensated for by the increased demand they can thus confer on themselves. Salop and Scheffman (1983) showed that there are many theoretical situations in which the profitability condition is satisfied. In fact, it is no doubt relatively less expensive for a firm to increase its rivals' costs than to use a limit-price policy in which the firm applying the policy risks loosing as much if not more (as a result of a larger size) than its rivals.

This brings me to consider the role of *price* as a strategic variable. With certainty, applying a price that is lower than the level that would maximize profits is not a credible signal to the entrant if, moreover, certain irreversibilities in production do not exist. We saw in section 4.2 that, according to Sylos-Labini's postulate, potential rivals assume that incumbents will maintain quantities corresponding to the lower price after their entry, hence rendering entry nonprofitable a priori. But, in fact, if entry actually takes place, it is in the interest of incumbents to reduce their output level in order to slow down the resulting fall in price. And because price/quantity policy is reversible, it is not clear what would prevent incumbents from acting in accordance with their self-interest. In the perfect equilibrium context the decision of potential entrants will not take the threat of limit price into consideration.

The situation changes radically, however, when *incomplete information* is introduced.[18] Fixing the price at a level different from the temporary monopolist's price is a credible signal likely to prevent entry or to reduce its probability for candidates who are imperfectly informed on the monopolist's demand curve or its cost funtion. Given the asymmetry in information, an intertemporal link is created between price/output applied before entry and expected behavior after entry. Price policy becomes an investment policy for making a reputation. Assume, for example, that the candidate for entry has perfect information except with regard to the incumbent's unit cost.[19] The incumbent could clearly "innocently" apply its monopoly price, ignoring the threat of entry and thus allowing the potential rival to infer its cost from this. Otherwise, knowing that the entrant has incomplete information, it can try to mislead the entrant; it could, for instance, reduce its price to make it seem as if its costs are low (that it is efficient) and thus discourage entry.[20] When there is only one period, the potential rival can attribute only an a priori probability to each possible state. Define ω as the probability that the rival will be confronted with an efficient incumbent, $\pi_E < 0$ as the corresponding entry profit, and $\pi_I > 0$ as the rival's profit if it encounters an inefficient firm. For the entrant to renounce entry, it is clearly sufficient that its subjectively expected profit be negative:

$$\omega\pi_E + (1 - \omega)\pi_I < 0,$$

which implies

$$\omega > \pi_I/\pi_I - \pi_E).$$

If the game is played over two periods, the monopolist will choose in the first period a price that depends on its costs. The entrant, with its own a priori probabilities, observes this price and corrects its own according to a Bayesian process by developing an a posteriori probability distribution on the incumbent's costs. The entrant then compares its expected profits if it enters (evaluated on the basis of the a posteriori distribution) with the zero profits corresponding to no entry. The incumbent can equally infer from the price it has chosen in the first period the decision regarding entry. The difficulty is then to specify the entrant's beliefs for each price level in the first period. A more general concept of equilibrium is used for this type of game, namely, *perfect Bayesian equilibrium*, or sequential equilibrium (see, in particular, Kreps and Wilson (1982)).

Most of the strategic weapons mentioned so far occur again when we analyze the phenomenon of *exit*. A basic question concerning this phenomenon is, Who goes first? When there are exit barriers, an exit that is potentially profitable to the industry may be rejected, even if every firm is aware of this positive effect. The problem is illustrated in figure 4.6, in which the exit game is defined as a "war of attrition."[21] The corresponding market is assumed to have shrunk to the point at which only one firm can operate profitably while two firms currently occupy the market.

If both firms in figure 4.6 remain in the market, each gets R, and if both exit, each obtains S. If one firm remains and the other leaves, the remaining firm has T. Given the existence of exit barriers, it can be assumed that $T > R > S$.

		Firm 2	
		Exit	Remain
Firm 1	Exit	(S, S)	(S, T)
	Remain	(T, S)	(R^*, R^*)

Figure 4.6
Exit game.

Then neither firm will exit although it is socially desirable that one of them do so. For example, firm 1 will remain if it believes that firm 2 will exit ($T > S$), but it will also remain if it expects firm 2 to remain ($R > S$). In fact, remaining is the dominant strategy for both firms. By enlarging the strategy space of the game, we can use various means to modify such a result. The first aspect is the role of competition by predation. Some incumbents have important financial resources at their disposal, coming, for instance, from other markets, and once entry has taken place, they can impose losses on the entrant, and their own losses are more than compensated for by the dissuasive effect exerted on potential future rivals. Thus they prompt the exit or the absorption of these firms. The incumbents themselves can exert barriers to their own exit when the cost of the corresponding investment is more than compensated for by the gain arising from the dissuasive effect on entry: Indeed high barriers to exit form a signal to potential rivals that incumbents intend to stay in place and maintain their level of activity after entry. At most, if all the costs of incumbents were sunk, entrants would be constrained to adopt Sylos-Labini's postulate, because a reduction in output level would not change these costs.

It can be concluded from these remarks that barriers to entry and exit are closely interdependent. From the incumbents' point of view, the higher the strategic barriers to exit, the less the necessity of barriers to entry. But equally, investments in the form of specific and durable assets reduce flexibility and increase the difficulty of leaving the industry during a crisis. There is a delicate tradeoff between the adoption of irreversible commitments and the safeguard of a minimum of flexibility, and this tradeoff lies at the heart of the set of strategic choices.

From the viewpoint of potential entrants, the presence of barriers to exit affecting all activity within the industry is likely to work in their favor. These collective barriers counter barriers to entry because, once in place, the newcomers have a strong motive to stay and, moreover, because predatory policies become inefficient. One possible industrial configuration is then a market with little exit and heavy entry, implying a tendency to deconcentration.

This interdependence between entry and exit conditions also suggests the importance of the concept of *mobility barriers* (Caves and Porter 1977). The basic idea is that in the same industry there exist differentiated groups of firms that have distinct objectives, resources, and strategies (large multinational groups, specialized domestic enterprises, conglomerates, etc.). The recognition of such *intra-industrial variations* among strategic groups suggests three things. First, the attempt at entry will generally be focused not on an industry as a whole but on a particular group in the industry, chosen on the basis of a comparison of mutual resources. Second, entry will be sequential; rather than a drastic contrast of games before and after entry, the phenomenon of entry is a gradual process leading to the successive occupation of the domain of activity of various groups within the same industry.[22] Finally, the notion of mobility barriers widens the use of the concept of barriers to the domain of competition between actual rivals. The incumbents' more or less irreversible investments not only are concerned with potential rivals but are equally aimed at reducing the possibilities of profit making for the other firms in the market. Through the accumulation of specific resources for which the markets are imperfect or inexistent, through the use of policies of control or manipulation of information, and through the adoption of organizational systems that tie up suppliers or buyers, firms tend to reduce cross elasticities among themselves and to make any move from one strategic group to another costly.

4.5 Process of Domination and Limits of Rationality

The preceding discussion has brought to light the various strategic possibilities available to economic agents in their relations with the industrial environment. Two major problems affect the modeling, however: assumed asymmetry and postulated rationality.

Most models of strategic competition[23] rest on the *hypothesis of initial asymmetry*. In situations in which having the initiative is advantageous (there is rivalry to act first) and in which information is perfect, incumbents are favored by asymmetry before entry; they are assumed to have the initiative, and, thanks to the various policies evoked in section 4.4, they can make prior irrevocable commitments corresponding to credible threats. If, on the other hand, information is incomplete, one can do without a priori arguments giving incumbents the power to take the initiative. On the contrary, the usual hypothesis made is asymmetry in information: Potential rivals are generally assumed to suffer from lack of information on the preferences, space of strategies, and costs of their adversaries already established in the market, whereas the converse is not true. A functional relationship then emerges endogenously between the actions of the incumbents and those of the entrants, showing that it is rational for informed firms to adopt policies of preemption and predation in order to consolidate their reputation.

To go beyond this type of a priori hypothesis, it would be necessary to revert to a more historic perspective of the process of domination—a perspective based on a sequence of pregames and games in which previous experience, acquired reputation, and anticipation interact. One way of conceiving of this process is to start from the idea that signals emanating from the markets indicate the possibility of profitable activities. Among the whole set of possible economic agents, some firms decide to inquire and turn into players. These players will then carry out several attempts to enter in some activities or some markets. From this generation of trials some will be successful, in the sense that in situations in which the order of actions matters, some players will have moved according to the most advantageous order. According to the characteristics of the situation, it is indeed preferable either to go first, reducing the choices left to one's followers, or to play second, forcing the other to take the risks inherent to the pioneer, and to widen the possibilities of choice for one's followers.[24] The outcome will be the entry into a market or an activity of a firm benefiting from the order of movement. Such a firm will exploit this advantage, which will generate favorable outcomes, allowing in turn the creation of a dominant position through various forms of irreversible commitments. Finally, from such a dominant position the firm can undertake investments that reinforce its position and make it persist over time. Figure 4.7 illustrates this process of domination (Geroski and Jacquemin 1984).[25]

An important aspect of this perspective is that many asymmetries arise at each stage of the decision process. The asymmetries are linked to the features of the game's stages: differences in perception, aptitude, attitude toward risk, temporal horizon. Moreover, asymmetry at a given level affects behavior and conditions of action in following games. In contrast to the implications of the case in which agents and players are identical or capable of imitating each other perfectly and without costs or are engaged in "races" independent of their characteristics, the concept emerging from this view is that of strategist firms that by force or by bluff try to control in a dynamic process their rivals and their environment to their own advantage. They calculate, anticipate, and invest in irreversible capital, thus

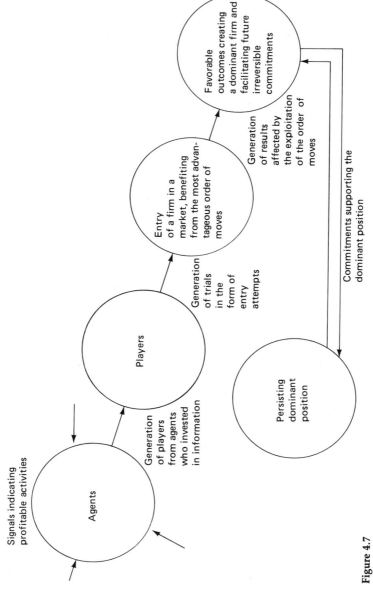

Figure 4.7
Process of creating a dominant position.

segmenting markets, increasing their rivals' costs, tying up their suppliers and their clients, and manipulating information.

But such a complex approach raises a crucial question: Doesn't the (not indispensible) requirement that corresponding behaviors be optimizing, that is, be derived as optimal strategies at equilibrium, demand an *excessive* degree of rationality?

In section 4.4 the concept of a perfect Bayesian equilibrium was briefly evoked with regard to a situation in which the entrant is unaware of the costs of the incumbent; however, the underlying rationality appears extreme. Indeed the entry candidate is assumed to be capable of imagining all possible cost structures of its adversary and of attributing a subjective probability to all eventualities; of calculating the likelihood of the price strategy used by its rival as a function of each cost structure $c_1, \ldots, c_j, \ldots, c_n$; of estimating the joint probability to have at the same time a cost structure c_j and a price policy p for each possible cost structure; of evaluating the marginal probability of having this price policy p, whatever the cost structure; and finally of assessing the posterior probability of the cost structure affecting its rival.[26] It is only after consideration of these points that the entrant can discover its best response. Even by adopting simplifying hypotheses, which are liable to bias the results strongly (only one decision variable, only one incumbent, a rigid sequence of entries), the entrant is still led rapidly to highly sophisticated models that call for an exceptional capacity for calculation, inference from past, and anticipation from the actors. The complexity is further increased if consumers are included among the rational players.[27]

Moreover, even if we assume such superrationality, we are far from being certain of obtaining precise results that may confer a predictive power to such models. The num-

ber of possible noncooperative equilibria for a given structure is generally large, without any clear criterion of choice
among them. Furthermore, the solutions are not robust,
for they are sensitive to slight modifications in assumed
initial conditions. Finally, any behavior can be rational-
ized, in particular by playing with information conditions
(see note 16).

These limits are perhaps the price we pay for having at
our disposal tools of analysis that allow a description of
strategic relations among economic agents. They suggest
the need for richer structures of models that should incor-
porate more economic, social, and institutional characteristics. Collaboration with other means of approaching this
problem appear equally indispensible, whether it is the
"behaviorist" conception or case studies based on comparative and historic methods. Otherwise, the question of
firms' strategies risks becoming, like some other economic
problems, a pretext for subtle but futile school exercises.

In the behaviorist perspective, some authors radically
question the hypothesis of optimizing behavior, irrespective of whether it is based on some kind of evolutionary
mechanism or a postulate justified by its fecundity. Moreover, they believe that the concern for giving an account of
observed industrial configurations by resorting to notions
of long-run equilibrium is not interesting.

The first aspect has been mainly explored by Simon
(1978, 1979), who has shown that decision makers systematically restrict the acquisition and utilization of information compared to what is available. Simon's criterion of
satisfaction is in fact based on a retroactive mechanism
between what he calls a subjective level of aspiration and
the scale of information judged necessary to attain this
level. Firms are then supposed to obey a limited or "pro-
cedural" rationality, the axiomatic basis of which is not
defined. Rather than adopting optimal actions, firms

choose procedures that are adapted to recurring questions most often met, given the complexity of the environment and the limits of the cognitive power of the human spirit:[28] The result is a predominance of customary rules, routine behavior, customs, and tradition. One application of this approach is that of Radner and Rothschild (1975). According to them, managers facing complex situations in which they must allocate their efforts among many activities are unable to formulate a complete preference ordering over the set of all possible outcomes of the process, to find corresponding optimal strategies, and to follow these. Radner and Rothschild then derived the properties of some rules of behavior that managers could in a more plausible manner adopt in order to allocate their (limited) efforts. Activities toward which efforts are devoted are assumed to tend to improve, whereas those that are neglected tend to deteriorate. Three types of rules are considered: a proportional allocation of effort among activities that is constant over time; an allocation of all the effort at any time to the activities that realize the worst performances at that time; and an allocation of all the effort at any time to activities with the best payoffs at that time. The main result is that, in general, the payoff of different activities does not tend toward a stationary regime. For his part, Lesourne (1979) laid the foundations for an integrated theory of individual behavior that answers the needs of economic analysis while being compatible with propositions coming from other human sciences, psychology in particular. Optimizing behavior in this context is considered a limiting case of an adaptative behavior.

Another pioneering work is relevant to the second aspect regarding equilibrium. This is the approach adopted by Schumpeter. For Schumpeter competition is a dynamic process from which new combinations arise and in which some firms win, partly by chance and partly by adoption of a good strategy. Only actual experience can determine who has placed a good or a bad bet, and it is not possible to explore adequately such a process with a model that assumes that the "contest" is totally defined and leads to equilibrium. Schumpeter put forward his conception in his *Theory of Economic Development* (1912). After having asserted that Darwinian theories of social evolution are discredited in the matter, Schumpeter declared:

Evolution is a phenomenon totally alien to what is observed in a circular flow or tendency towards equilibrium. It concerns discontinuous and spontaneous changes in flow channels, a disorder in equilibrium that alters this irreversibly. (ch. 2)

In the sphere of production, such an evolution appears by the introduction of a new product, a new quality, or a new method of production, by the opening of new markets and new sources of supply, and finally "by the implementation of a new industrial organization, such as the creation of a monopoly position through a network of trusts" (Schumpeter 1912, ch. 2).

Similar to the work of J. B. Clarck, M. Weber, and W. Sombart, the Schumpeterian conception is therefore that of an economy that cannot remain stationary and that is constantly revolutionized from within by new initiatives.[29]

One can consider that the studies of Schumpeter and Simon have been combined in the *evolutionary theory of economic change* put forward by Nelson and Winter (1982). This theory is opposed to a system in which optimizing agents interact in such a way that they are close to an equilibrium and can follow, rapidly and with precision, any change in equilibrium. On the contrary, economic agents are assumed to behave in accordance with "routine rules." If these rules evolve, it is through a search process that is never exhaustive, in the sense that for a given time period only a fraction of the set of possible routines is examined. In other respects, although equations of movement are defined, no reference is made to any kind of stationary equilibrium. The central but not exclusive role is played by stochastic processes, and the models used frequently resort to various formulations of Gibrat's law.[30] The process of concentration in an industry thus depends not only on the initial degree of dispersion but also on difficulties of imitation encountered by firms that have not innovated and the expansion of capital stock of firms that enjoy a higher level of productivity and profitability. The resulting stationary regime corresponds more to some kind of statistical regularity than to customary conceptions of long-term equilibrium.

By incorporating the role of entrants as sources of innovation, Winter (1984) extended the Nelson-Winter Markovian model of a single industry in which existing firms produce a homogeneous product and in which cost reduction through internal productivity improvement is the major competitive weapon. Entry, however, is not conceived in a strategic fashion in which identified actors act on the basis of close calculations of prospective returns. The possibility of entry is based on some background or external research and development activity that is relevant to the industry's technology but is not funded by the industry itself. Entry then occurs through a random process according to which certain firms draw innovation while others draw imitation.

Concluding this section, I must stress that the studies of Nelson and Winter in no way constitute support for the evolutionary approach as it was evoked in chapter 2. On the contrary, they are opposed to any attempt to found the hypothesis of profit maximization and the prediction of the predominance of efficient industrial configurations on selection mechanisms.

Radical assertions that the forces of economic selection lead individual firms and global systems to optimal behavior cannot be defended by appending a plausible genetic mechanism. There is no reason to believe that the usual reactions of existing firms include the set of reactions which are best with regards to a wider range of possibilities.[31] (Nelson and Winter 1982, p. 142)

Rather, what these studies suggest is the necessity to be more open to an evolutionary perspective in which the competitive process is more important than equilibrium and in which cumulative interactions among economic agents' vast strategy space and industrial structure have no chance of leading to an optimum.

Notes

1. Recall that in control theory, control variables depend only on time ("open-loop strategy") or on time and state variables ("closed-loop strategy"). In the second situation a player can at any time observe the state of the system and react to it. Even then, however, the feedback laws are defined a priori, before the start of the game, and cannot be modified over time.

2. The same result is obtained when introducing a market demand that increases over time (Ireland 1972). Rather than the disappearance of the dominant firm, it seems more plausible to envisage the possibility of a change of regime, when the market share of the "dominant firm" is below a certain threshold. Then the form of the market (the type of equilibrium) could, for example, shift from a Stackelberg type of asymmetric situation to a symmetric competitive form in which the previously leading firm becomes a competitor among the others. This type of change of regime has been formalized by Encaoua et al. (1981).

3. See particularly Baumol et al. (1982) but also Grossman (1981), who builds a model in which decision variables are no longer quantities but supply functions.

4. See the various types enumerated by Ordover and Willig (1981). Note that the existence of a rental market may reduce sunk costs if it increases mobility and fungibility of durable goods between alternative *usages*.

5. For a more systematic analysis, see Weitzman (1983), according to whom one cannot have in a single-product case decreasing average cost over a certain range without sunk costs.

6. For developments, see Encaoua and Jacquemin (1980).

7. In particular, optimal control theory in its usual form must be abandoned, insofar as firms' strategies are calculated at time zero and their reexamination at time t is excluded. Intertemporal policies determined in this way are likely to be inconsistent if the optimal policy, evaluated at time zero and determining expansion paths for the control variables (dependent on time or on a state variable), implies values for the control variables at time t that would not be optimal if policy were reviewed at this time (see Kydland and Prescott (1977)). This problem of time consistency can be partly resolved by resorting to the notion of irrevocable investment, which excludes (or makes too costly) future deviations from the initial plan, and by using the concept of perfect equilibrium requiring an optimal choice at each time period. This last concept corresponds to a "perfect closed-loop equilibrium," in which each firm regularly reevaluates its actions in the light of new information concerning the realized actions of its rivals and, when reevaluating, adopts a plan that is optimal for the remainder of the game. Subsequent sections examine these approaches.

8. Profit functions are obtained supposedly after substitution of equilibrium price in terms of the level of capital. Capital is assumed to appear in the cost function. Note that the incumbent does not automatically hold the initiative in the various possible strategies. On the contrary, it may happen that at a given moment the incumbent is surprised by the appearance of a candidate for entry and by the entrant's investment in such a way that the incumbent is forced to respond to this initiative. For this case, see Tirole (1983).

9. The possibility of prior communication is clearly essential for firms to be able to use threats. As we will see, this communication makes some Nash equilibria unstable. See d'Aspremont and Gerard-Varet (1980) and Moulin (1981).

10. Note, however, that the potential competition has reduced the profits that firm 1 would have obtained in monopoly equilibrium. The maximization of monopolist's profits $\pi_1 = K_1 - K_1^2$ leads in fact to the same optimal level of capital, $K_1 = \frac{1}{2}$, and to a higher level of equilibrium profits, $\pi_1 = \frac{1}{4}$.

11. For instance, if $F = 1/20$, then $K_1 = 1 - 2\sqrt{1/20} = 0.55$ and $\pi_1 = 0.247$. In figure 4.4 the reaction function of firm 2 is discontinuous at K in the sense that at this level both the profits and the capital of firm 2 are equal to zero.

12. For extensions of the concept of perfect equilibrium, see Kreps and Wilson (1982), who put forward the notion of sequential equilibrium. In their particularly complex formalization any perfect equilibrium is sequential, but the inverse is not true.

13. See Dixit (1982) and Encaoua et al. (1986).

14. Reasoning by backward induction is the general method used in games with a finite horizon. It corresponds to a procedure of eliminating dominated decisions (that is, there is a decision available that gives a higher gain irrespective of future events), decomposing the game into subgames, and resolving the subgames by starting from the end of the tree until one resolves a game without subgames. On the other hand, when the horizon is infinite, other methods must be used.

15. Formally, this would be the case if $(\pi_d - \pi_g)_{t_0} < \Sigma_{t=1}^{T} (\pi_m - \pi_d)\gamma$, where γ is the discount factor.

16. Note that this paradox is also an argument to show that in the case of the *prisoner's dilemma*, the unique Nash equilibrium will correspond to the adoption of noncooperative strategies. When information is complete, the player who plays last would be well advised to adopt a noncooperative behavior because the other player will not have the occasion to retaliate. But the other player aware of this would do well to adopt a noncooperative strategy at the previous stage. For the game to have an equilibrium in which the dominant strategies correspond to cooperation, it should either be repeated indefinitely, with a discount factor that is sufficiently close to 1, or be repeated in a finite manner but with uncertainty about the end of the game. In the first case each player maximizes its own discounted stream of profits, $\pi_i = \Sigma_{t=1} \gamma^{t-1}\pi_t^i$, where $\gamma = 1/(1 + r)$ is the discount factor. It is well known that if γ is close to 1, any individual rational outcome can be sustained as a credible Nash equilibrium of the repeated game. This is the so-called folk theorem. In the second case, γ is interpreted as the probability that the game will continue into the next period. If this probability is sufficiently high, any individual rational outcome can again be sustained, and many noncooperative outcomes are possible.

17. For a more complete survey, see Encaoua et al. (1986) and Geroski and Jacquemin (1984). Von Weizsacker (1980) analyzed this question in the light of social welfare.

18. Recall that information is imperfect when players are unaware of their rivals' earlier moves, wheras information is incomplete when players do not know the precise characteristics of their rivals, in particular, their cost conditions. Here the distinction is not important. The notion of a game with incomplete information was introduced by Harsanyi (1967–1968).

19. See, in particular, studies by Milgrom and Roberts (1982a, 1982b) and by Fudenberg and Tirole (1986).

20. Conversely, the incumbent could try to persuade the potential rival that it is weak, that is, that the market aimed at by the rival is structurally nonprofitable: The incumbent will again resort to low price, but now this reaction should be interpreted opposite to the way in the text. For a model of this type, see Easley et al. (1981).

21. A war of attrition has the rule that the winner of a contest is the contestant prepared to continue the longest. In an asymmetric war of attrition, opponents differ in their relative persistence potential and the value of winning. See also chapter 3, note 36.

22. A typical example is entry by means of production of bottomline quality and a progressive extension toward high-quality production.

23. Among exceptions, see Flaherty (1980a), who presents a model in which the initial situation confronting firms is symmetric, that is, identical for all. She then shows that there exist both symmetric and asymmetric stationary equilibria, but only the latter are stable.

24. The field of new technologies, particularly computing, illustrates this kind of situation particularly well. The choice between strategies of innovation or imitation is often crucial (see Freeman (1974), ch. 7).

25. The study referred to develops various aspects of this process.

26. Bayes's theorem allows the calculation of the posterior probability $P_0(c_j|\bar{p})$ of the "state of nature" c_j, given that p is the price applied, based on prior probabilities and the observation of p. It is written

$P_0(c_j|\bar{p}) = [P(c_j \text{ and } p)]/P(\bar{p}),$

where $P(c_j \text{ and } p)$ is the joint probability and $P(\bar{p})$ is the marginal probability.

27. Bulow (1982) analyzed the case of consumers with rational expectations confronting producers of durable goods. He showed how a seller of such goods may attempt to convince buyers able to realize that price-skimming policies may not be consistent over time that future production will be limited. This is done through self-enforcing precommitments, such as investing less in plant modernization and research and development activities than it would do otherwise. Notice that these strategies could lead to perverse effects for potential competition.

28. Trying to redefine the search for a level of satisfaction as a special case of a maximizing behavior, when information costs have been taken into account, clashes with the objection that we are then led to an unending backward induction. Indeed the choice of an information structure consistent with profit maximization requires information, and the way in which the maximizing candidate is to acquire this information is not defined.

29. Among various discussions of Schumpeter's thought, see Perroux (1965).

30. The basic principle is that, if the firm population is constant and if the rates of growth of firms period by period are generated by probability distributions that are independent among firms and that are identical for all firms over all periods (implying, in particular, the absence of any systematic relation between size of firms and the distribution of their rate of growth), then the distribution of the size of firms will approximate a log-normal distribution.

31. This view is sustained by Iwai (1984) on the basis of a simple evolutionary model in which there are dynamic interactions between the equilibrating force of imitation and the disequilibrating force of innovation. It is shown that the industry will never approach a neoclassical equilibrium with perfect knowledge even in the long run and that instead there will be a relative dispersion of efficiency across firms. "The blind force of economic selection is outwitted by the human force of innovative activities" (Iwai 1984, p. 347).

References

W. Baumol, J. Panzar, and R. Willig. 1982. *Contestable Markets and the Theory of Industry Structure*. New York: Harcourt Brace Jovanovich.

F. Bourguignon and S. Sethi. 1981. "Dynamic optimal pricing and (possibly) advertising in the face of various kinds of potential entrants." *Journal of Economic Dynamics and Control* 3:119–140.

J. Bulow. 1982. "Durable goods monopolists." *Journal of Political Economy* 90(2):314–332.

R. Caves and M. Porter. 1977. "From entry barriers to mobility barriers: Conjectural decisions and contrived deterrence to new competition." *Quarterly Journal of Economics* 91(2):241–261.

P. Dasgupta and J. Stiglitz. 1980. "Industrial structure and the nature of innovative activity." *Economic Journal* 90:266–293.

C. d'Aspremont and L. A. Gerard-Varet. 1980. "Sincere pre-play communication and Stackelberg competitive games." *Journal of Economic Theory* 23:201–217.

R. de Bondt. 1977. "On the effects of retarded entry." *European Economic Review* 9:361–371.

A. Dixit. 1982. "Recent developments in oligopoly theory." *American Economic Review* 72(2):12–17.

D. Easley, R. Masson, and R. Reynolds. 1981. "A dynamic analysis of predatory pricing with rational expectations." Department of Economics, Cornell University.

D. Encaoua and A. Jacquemin. 1980. "Degree of monopoly, indices of concentration and threat of entry." *International Economic Review* 21(1):87–105.

D. Encaoua, P. Geroski, and A. Jacquemin. 1986. "Strategic competition and the persistence of dominant firms: A survey," in *New Developments in the Analysis of Market Structure*, J. Stiglitz and F. Mathewson (eds.). Cambridge: The MIT Press, 55–86.

D. Encaoua, A. Jacquemin, and P. Michel. 1981. "Stratégies dynamiques de prix et structures de marché" (Dynamic price strategies and market structure). *Cahiers du Séminaire d'Econométrie* 23:153–168.

M. T. Flaherty. 1980a. "Dynamic limit pricing, barriers to entry and rational firms." *Journal of Economic Theory* 23:160–182.

M. T. Flaherty. 1980b. "Industry structure and cost-reducing investment." *Econometrica* 48(5):1187–1209.

C. Freeman. 1974. *The Economics of Industrial Innovation.* London: Penguin Books.

D. Fudenberg and J. Tirole. 1986. "Dynamic models of oligopoly," in *Fundamentals of Pure and Applied Economics,* A. Jacquemin (ed.). London: Harwood, 1–83.

D. Gaskins. 1971. "Dynamic limit pricing: Optimal pricing under threat of entry." *Journal of Economic Theory* 3:306–322.

P. Geroski and A. Jacquemin. 1984. "Dominant firms and their alleged decline." *International Journal of Industrial Organization* 2: 1–27.

S. Grossman. 1981. "Nash equilibrium and the industrial organization of markets with large fixed costs." *Econometrica* 49(5):1149–1172.

J. Harsanyi. 1967–1968. "Games with incomplete information played by 'Bayesian' players I–III." *Management Science* 14:159–182, 320–334, 486–502.

N. Ireland. 1972. "Concentration and the growth of market demand." *Journal of Economic Theory* 5:303–305.

K. Iwai. 1984. "Schumpeterian dynamics." *Journal of Economic Behavior and Organization* 5:121–151.

A. Jacquemin. 1967. *L'entreprise et son pouvoir de marché* (The firm and its market power). Paris: PUF.

A. Jacquemin. 1971. "Stratégie d'entreprise, structure de marché et contrôle optimal" (Strategy of the firm, market structure and optimal control). *Revue d'Economie Politique* 82:1104–1118.

A. Jacquemin and J. Thisse. 1972. "Strategy of the firm and market structure: An application of optimal control theory," in *Market Structure and Corporate Behaviour,* K. Cowling (ed.). London: Gray-Mills, 61–84.

M. Kamien and N. Schwartz. 1975. "Cournot oligopoly with uncertain entry." *Review of Economic Studies* 42:125–131.

D. Kreps and M. Spence. 1985. "Modelling the role of history in industrial organization and competition," in *Contemporary Issues in Modern Microeconomics*, G. Feiwal (ed.). London: Macmillan, 58–85.

D. Kreps and R. Wilson. 1982. "Sequential equilibria." *Econometrica* 50(4):863–894.

F. Kydland and E. Prescott. 1977. "Rules rather than discretion: The inconsistency of optimal plans." *Journal of Political Economy* 85(3):473–491.

W. Lee. 1975. "Oligopoly and entry." *Journal of Economic Theory* 11:25–38.

J. Lesourne. 1979. *A Theory of the Individual for Economic Analysis*. Amsterdam: North-Holland.

G. Loury. 1979. "Market structure and innovation." *Quarterly Journal of Economics* 93(3):395–410.

P. Milgrom and J. Roberts. 1982a. "Limit pricing and entry under incomplete information: An equilibrium analysis." *Econometrica* 50(5):1089–1122.

P. Milgrom and J. Roberts. 1982b. "Predation, reputation, and entry deterrence." *Journal of Economic Theory* 27:280–312.

H. Moulin. 1981. "Deterrence and cooperation: A classification of two-person games." *European Economic Review* 15:179–194.

R. Nelson and S. Winter. 1982. *An Evolutionary Theory of Economic Change*. Cambridge: Harvard University Press.

J. Ordover and R. Willig. 1981. "An economic definition of predation pricing and product innovation." *The Yale Law Journal* 1:8–53.

F. Perroux. 1965. *La penśee économique de Joseph Schumpeter, les dynamiques du capitalisme* (The economic thought of Joseph Schumpeter: The dynamics of capitalism). Paris: Droz.

R. Radner and R. Rothschild. 1975. "On the allocation of effort." *Journal of Economic Theory* 10:358–376.

J. Reinganum. 1982. "A dynamic game of R and D." *Econometrica* 50(3):671–688.

S. Salop and D. Scheffman. 1983. "Raising rivals' costs." *American Economic Review* 73(2):267–271.

T. Schelling. 1960. *The Strategy of Conflict*. Cambridge: Harvard University Press.

F. Scherer. 1980. *Industrial Market Structure and Economic Performance*. Chicago: Rand McNally.

J. Schumpeter. 1912 (1974). *The Theory of Economic Development*. Oxford: Oxford University Press.

R. Selten. 1975. "Re-examination of the perfectness concept for equilibrium points in extensive games." *International Journal of Game Theory* 4:25–55.

R. Selten. 1978. "The chain-store paradox." *Theory and Decision* 9:127–159.

H. Simon. 1978. "Rationality as process and as product of thought." *American Economic Review* 68(2):1–16.

H. Simon. 1979. "Rational decision making in business administration." *American Economic Review* 69(4):493–513.

G. Stigler. 1968. *The Organization of Industry*. Homewood, NJ: Irwin.

P. Sylos-Labini. 1957. *Oligopoly and Technical Progress*. Cambridge: Harvard University Press.

J. Tirole. 1985. *Concurrence imparfaite* (Imperfect competition). Paris: Economica.

C. von Weizsacker. 1980. *Barriers to Entry: Theoretical Treatment*. Berlin: Springer-Verlag.

M. Weitzman. 1983. "Contestable markets: An uprising in the theory of industry structure. Comment." *American Economic Review* 73(3):486–487.

S. Winter. 1984. "Schumpeterian competition in alternative technological regimes." *Journal of Economic Behavior and Organization* 5:287–320.

5   Organizational Forms and the Firm

For some time now the firm has not been considered as an abstract entity characterized simply by a production function and an objective function to maximize; rather, it is now viewed as a form of organization. The market and the enterprise are then alternative instruments, each having their advantages and their inconveniences for the allocation of resources.[1] A transaction would have to be realized through a relation among firms or through intrafirm operations according to costs and benefits of the organizations involved. More generally, hierarchies, federations of firms, and markets compete with each other to provide coordination, allocation, and monitoring. It is only when one organizational form promises for specific activities a higher net return than alternative institutional arrangements that it will survive in the long run.

In this general context we once again see the contrast between the two perspectives expounded in previous chapters. First, some researchers believe that processes of allocation that are "internalized" are those that would not be efficiently realized in a decentralized manner through market mechanisms: The existence of transaction costs linked to a set of factors, such as limited information and specificity of transactions, makes contracts complex and costly to draw up, execute, and control. Coupled with economies of production, transaction costs lead to the emergence of hierarchical organizations endowed with internal control. Among the possible structures of internal organization, the ones tending to predominate over time are those that ensure the minimization of such costs. According to Chandler (1977, 1982) and Williamson (1975, 1981), the optimal form from this point of view is the multidivisional form (M-form).

In contrast, other researchers believe that the choice of organizational structure, if dictated by the search for maximum profits, does not necessarily correspond to the "efficient" form. If such a structure is a strategic variable, then its choice is not determined simply by cost minimization: Indeed an additional organizational cost could be more than compensated for by the increase in revenue made possible by the better control of the market resulting from the adoption of this structure.

In section 5.1 I examine the characteristics of the M-form in the framework of firms minimizing their costs. In section 5.2 I investigate various existing organizational forms, both inter- and intrafirm, and the absence of their evolution toward a unique type. Finally, in the third section I envisage the role of organizational mode as a strategic decision variable.

5.1 Natural Organization of the Firm and M-Forms

In some circumstances a team (an organized group of agents who share a common utility function) has superiority over a set of bilateral transactions (Alchian and Demsetz 1972; Marschak and Radner 1972; Williamson 1975). For instance, for indivisibilities in the utilization of physical or informational assets, a collective property could be preferable to an individual one;[2] equally, problems of limited rationality are better met by the development of specialized codes within a team; opportunistic behavior, which usually affects situations in which the number of participants is small, is minimized through the identification of individuals to the organization and the sharing of common values.

We can then compare the relative efficiency of a hierarchy with that of a team. The main argument is that beyond a certain size the process of collective decision making associated with a team is more costly than that of a hierarchy. A first aspect is that the number of required channels of communication is much higher for a team and increases rapidly with the number of participants, whereas the hierarchy, which is based on a differentiation of status and behavior within the group, decreases this number.

In figure 5.1a each member of the team is assumed to communicate with its equal, which requires six channels of communication. In figure 5.1b w is the coordinator of the hierarchy, having the responsibility of communicating with the other three members of the group and making decisions on this basis; the number of channels is not more than three. For a number n of participants, the network of communication channels is equal to $n(n - 1)/2$ for a team and $(n - 1)$ for a hierarchy. More generally and except for small groups, the hierarchy recognizes that individual members do not necessarily identify themselves with the

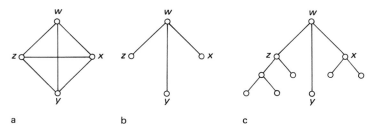

a   b   c

Figure 5.1
Channels of communication and organization.

organization to which they belong. Therefore the quality of decision making can be improved by confining it to the most competent; opportunistic behavior is avoided by setting up specialized and systematic control; if the conditions of action change, the time of reaction is limited through decentralized procedures.

Beyond a given size a hierarchy also encounters some difficulties. Given the limits of rationality and cognitive capacity, the central agent can coordinate only a limited number of channels. In figure 5.1c the central agent is supposed to control nine channels, whereas it is assumed to reach its saturation with three. Therefore the central agent should envisage division of responsibilities and delegation of supervision, as illustrated; the form of this division itself becomes crucial.

It is at this stage of *complex hierarchy* that the studies by Chandler and Williamson enable a contrast between two ideal types.[3] The unitary form (U-form) corresponds to a centralized multifunctional organization. The major active units are functional divisions in the sense that there is specialization by function. This organization a priori favors the realization of economies of scale and the internal division of labor (see figure 5.2). Nevertheless, this type of expansion, whether it results from increased activity in a

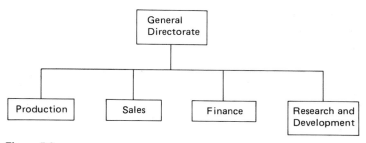

Figure 5.2
Unitary form of organization.

given line of products or from diversification, risks leading to important internal inefficiency, linked with a loss of control. Problems arise at the levels of determining objectives and of allocating resources internally. So far as determining objectives is concerned, there is the danger that managers, who are simultaneously responsible for long-term strategic decisions and daily operational decisions, will give more attention to the short run, because the pressures are more direct. Moreover, deficiencies in lateral coordination lead to the pursuit of secondary objectives, such as sales or finance, creating distortions with regard to the objective of global profits. Managers are indeed likely to be overconcerned with their functional goals.[4] Furthermore, for a given goal the problem of mobility of resources within the enterprise arises. Rather than an internal market (of capital, labor, and information), the U-form favors a pyramidal and bureaucratic hierarchy in which feudalism and ritualism tend to predominate.

In contrast, the M-form seems to have all the virtues. It is perceived as the final outcome of a selective process that favors increased internal efficiency.

The modern corporation is mainly to be understood as the product of a series of organisational innovations that have had the purpose and effects of economising on transaction costs. (Williamson 1981, p. 1537)

In this historic perspective the emergence and the actual predominance of the M-form reflect its superior efficiency relative to alternative forms, in particular, the U-form.

The organisation and operation of the large enterprise along the lines of the M-form favours goal pursuit and least-cost behavior more nearly associated with the neoclassical profit maximisation hypothesis than does the U-form organisational alternative[5] (Williamson 1975, p. 150)

The M-form indeed presents itself as a happy combination of decentralization and concentration. It is derived from a constitution of "natural decision units" (Williamson 1971, p. 356), in the sense that elements that are in intense interaction are combined in a division, whereas elements that are weakly interactive are separated. Operational divisions enjoy a large degree of autonomy and take their own risks in such a way that each division constitutes a quasi-firm, managed to achieve a specific objective. The quasi-firms are defined according to lines of products or geographic zones, and they have functional divisions that ensure their autonomy. This is shown in figure 5.3, where divisions A, B, and C are products or geographic markets.

Three characteristics of the M-form must be stressed. First, the distribution of tasks is such that the general directorate assisted by a board of managerial staff is in charge of strategic decisions, including planning of investments and allocation of global resources among operational divisions, whereas the responsibility of operational decisions itself is

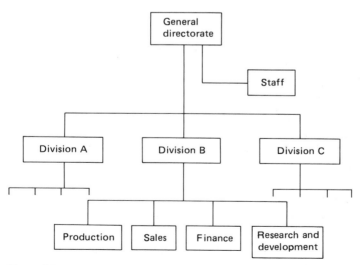

Figure 5.3
Multidivisional form of organization.

entrusted to line managers who run the divisions as profit centers. Second, the general directorate practices advisory functions as well as verification of accounts (internal audit), thus ensuring regular but not permanent control of different divisions. And third, the distinction between the general directorate and the operational divisions allows the general directorate to be concerned with the organization's general performance and to ensure compatibility between local results and global optimum.

At this stage, it is useful to reiterate that both economies in transaction costs and economies in production costs have a joint bearing on the choice of the organizational form of the enterprise.

We have seen the effect of economies of scale (section 2.2) on the phenomenon of *horizontal* concentration within the same industry. I should nevertheless explain the complementarity between effective realization of these technological economies and the quality of coordination within the enterprise. For instance, for a merger to reduce production costs, it might be necessary to divert production from an establishment suffering from inadequate capacity to another establishment that would thus attain its optimal minimal size. Such an effect can be obtained only by properly coordinating previously separated units, the flow of raw materials and finished products, and production techniques. This is even clearer for economies of scale at the level of the firm. The exploitation of such economies is a priori favored by a more refined internal organization, which allows in particular the allocation of some indivisible management services according to priorities, the coordination of interregional and international investments, the assurance of an efficient internal capital allocation, and the collective exploitation of some activities, such as research and development and technological know-how characterized as a public good. Hence, according to Chandler (1977,

1982), it is not surprising that the multidivisional structure is a predominant form of organization in industries characterized by economies linked with large size and high capital intensity.

The same complementarity between technological characteristics and organizational form is also found in *vertical* integration. Industries that are characterized by a close technological interdependence between successive stages of production and, moreover, that require a large volume of specific intermediate products or services are a priori designated for operations of vertical integration. Because of the necessities for recurrent transactions with specialized suppliers (benefiting from accumulated experience), strict quality control, delivery according to a precise frequency, and utilization of complex information under uncertainty and, more generally, because of close cooperation between users and suppliers, market mechanisms become rather inefficient: The cost of changing a client or a supplier could be prohibitive because of the specificity of the intermediate activity in question. Internalization of operations in the form of a hierarchy then becomes a plausible alternative.[6]

Finally, similar reasoning could be applied to *conglomerates*. We have seen (section 2.2) the roles of "economies of scope" and complementarity among products. From the moment when it is less costly to produce a set of goods jointly rather than separately, a joint product firm is considered a less costly form of organization than a single-product firm. For two products, if

$$c(y_1, y_2) < c(y_1, 0) + c(0, y_2),$$

all market structure comprising specialized firms will be unstable, that is, it would be profitable for them to merge. But again, in order to exploit these economies of scope based on common utilization of some goods and services,[7] the organizational structure of the diversified firm must be adapted: By combining highly interdependent units into divisions (the units' common characteristics being manifested in terms of products or spatial locality), the M-form leads to operational decisions being made at the level of these "natural" divisions.[8]

In conclusion, the emergence of a large, multidivisional, integrated, and diversified enterprise is supposed to reflect the importance of considerations regarding both technological and transaction costs. It is the joint existence that incites, first, a hierarchy and then a particular form of hierarchy, namely, the M-form. On this basis the large enterprise fulfills the requirement of the efficient allocation of resources and is even a necessary condition for this efficiency. In a framework of evolution, market forces select those who, by the choice of their organizational structure, minimize their costs. Williamson and Ouchi (1983) did not hesitate to give a deadline to such an evolution. They asserted: "If observations are made over sufficiently long intervals, say ten years, considerations of market power give their place to efficiency" (p. 67).

5.2 Polymorphism of Organizational Modes

I suggested in the previous section that certain organizational forms are likely to predominate because of their aptitude to minimize different types of cost. In this section I first discuss the coexistence at a given moment of time of various organizational structures and the absence of a net evolution toward certain types; then I question the idea that the perimeter of an enterprise can be determined simply by examining the underlying cost function.

A general remark is that there is a whole range of possible organizational modes that in no way can be reduced to a choice between the market and the firm and, at the firm level, between the U-form and the M-form. A first step in widening the range of organizational structures to be considered is to introduce *interfirm relations* between market relations and intrafirm organization. I can then discuss a continuum of *organizational structures* ranging from short-term contracts to total (legal) merger and including long-term contracts, the contractual group of the "economic joint venture" type, minority or majority shareholding, and quasi-integration.[9]

Two principles are likely to ensure the coordination of decisions between members of a group: management in the form of hierarchy and rules governing an association. Interfirm relations relate to the second type. Although in the United States interfirm organizations are rare, they are abundant in Japan and Europe and contribute to horizontal concentration, vertical integration, and diversification. In this case of interfirm relations, coordination is ensured by a set of more or less restrictive rules. Some rules are even tacit and informal; they emerge from a long history of exchange of information, financial relations, and collaboration leading to the recognition of mutual dependence. A typical example is such Japanese groups as Mitsui, Mitsubishi, Sumitomo, and Fuji, who are successors of the famous Zaibatsus. The Zaibatsus were groups of companies characterized by the inexistence of a central decision unit and the absence of important financial or personal dependency. On the other hand, the Zaibatsus constituted genuine clubs within which information was exchanged, especially information related to new investment projects, and major transactions of intermediate products took place. Relations within many European holdings and enterprises are of this nature.[10]

One can then defend that these intermediary forms are not simply transitory inefficient forms; they are under certain conditions likely to reduce the transaction costs that would have been incurred had the transaction taken place through the market and, at the same time, to avoid certain organizational costs that would have arisen had the transaction been totally internalized within the firm. Indeed market mechanism is not always an efficient medium for the production and the transmission of information characterized by increasing productivity (Wilson 1975), strong externalities, and difficulty in appropriation. Moreover, transactions among a small number of suppliers and consumers involving specified intermediate goods and requiring steady supplies over time correspond to contractual provisions not easily enforced. Also, many markets are imperfect or nonexistent, such as in the case of contingent contracts. On the other hand, complete internalization of these operations bears an equally high cost of internal administration in terms of both hierarchical rigidity and fixed working capital. The exploitation of the degree of interdependence between activities may then be ensured through more flexible and less heavy cooperation, such as that established within the Japanese "club of firms." In other words, the inadequacy of a pure market relationship based on buying and selling does not lead to the conclusion that total internalization of the operation is necessary; rather it opens the choice over the many intermediate possibilities that are different combinations of market mechanisms and administrative procedures. Thus for economies of scope Teece (1980) showed convincingly that, contrary to the remarks by Panzar and Willig (1975), the simple fact that the cost function manifests such economies is neither a necessary nor a sufficient condition for an enterprise to be diversified. The simultaneous production of the goods in question by a single firm is not necessarily less costly, and nonhierarchical forms of organization, including, for example, rental contracts, are likely to permit common utilization of indivisible input by many firms, who in other respects remain producers of a single product. The same argument applies to vertical integration. Not only is technological interdependence between successive stages of production insufficient for explaining vertical integration (Williamson 1975) but also transaction costs linked with phenomena of limited rationality and uncertainty[11] do not make it any easier to determine which is the efficient organizational structure for exploiting vertical interdependence. Establishing a particular form, such as the M-form, that is superior to all other forms, such as a long-term contract, a buying and stocking joint venture, a quasi-integration, or an association of the Zaibatsu type, requires such a restrictive specification of transaction costs that its formulation is implausible.

Finally, trying to determine optimal modes of organization simply on the basis of production and transaction costs is utopian. The organizational structure reflects the existence of a hierarchy as much in relations among firms as in coordinated activities within a firm and accommodates the various forces present, from inertia associated with the existing organization to pressures of external competition that induce modifications in the portfolio of activities.

The future of the firm depends on its competitive positioning and its organisational capacity to coordinate the remaining subgroups, both at the internal and external level. (Ponssard 1984)

This perspective is the more justified as changes in environmental conditions once again question certain organizational types and make it impossible to discern an irreversible evolution toward one or the other.

The crisis that has shed some light on the difficulties of adaptation and change facing large firms has from this point of view been revealing. Although the M-form evolved to counter bureaucratic inefficiency in large enterprises, this mode of organization has itself become the source of another problem. In order to supervise and direct the various operational divisions engaged in different activities, financial control, which is based on the common denominator of monetary return, has taken a dominant position in the organization, whereas the importance of managers specialized in marketing, technology, and human resources has declined. This evolution has resulted in an excessive weight being given to financial criteria; the result is abuse of mechanical methods of discounting (unfavorable to investments in human resources and in technology) and management of the activity portfolio that duplicates the management of the financial portfolio, excessively minimizing risk taking and favoring rapid returns.[12] It is not surprising, therefore, that new types of organizational structure have been sought for situations in which entrepreneurial quality is more than ever identified with the capacity to adapt to exogenous uncertainty in a flexible and innovative manner.

Recent studies on Japanese enterprise (Aoki 1984) contrast in this framework a "quasi-tree" structure with a tree form. Contrary to the tree structure (which characterizes the large multidivisional enterprise), the new form is based on "quasi-disintegration," which is decided by the large firms themselves.[13] These firms create affiliates by laying off their own managers and by encouraging them to organize, autonomously, legal entities. Contractual relations are then established between these and the initial company. These relations are characterized by various cavalcades, in the sense that the smaller innovative companies make contracts not only with the mother company but also with companies outside the group. Similarly, the mother company looks for contractors and subcontractors both inside and outside the group periphery. So far as research and innovation are concerned, initiative is not unidirectional, from the trunk to the main branches and then to the twigs, but works in all directions, from the summit to the base. Finally, quasi-disintegration encourages the formation of specific structures regarding employment and management of human resources. According to Aoki (1984), for large Japanese firms one of the major motives for quasi-disintegration is to make the management of industrial relations more flexible and adaptable to changing conditions. Quasi-disintegration reflects the need for decentralization and localization of the management of human resources.

It is not clear that such an organizational mode as quasi-disintegration is necessarily more efficient than M-forms. The resulting wide dispersion of risks and responsibilities opens the door in particular to problems of duplication and lack of global perspective. The object of the Japanese example is to show that in an environment of rapid evolution it would be wrong to believe that the best forms have been identified once and for all. The reality is a tangle of various forms—multidivisional, unitary, or others—in proportions that will evolve according to external conditions and the degree of rigidity of existing internal structures. In view of such a diversity it would be a tautology to consider all observed form as that minimizing cost, given the particular circumstances affecting each industry and each firm: It is indeed always possible to justify any organizational structure in terms of efficiency by resorting to ad hoc hypotheses. On the other hand, no theory of competition among organizational forms exists that enables us to assert that long-run equilibrium will be characterized by technologically efficient forms.

5.3 Organizational Forms and Market Strategies

Until now, the criterion of cost minimization has been kept for the discussion of the organizational form. But in the context of the theory of the firm, it is profit maximization that should be adopted.

The starting point of this section is the following: Not only is there a well-recognized link running from market activities to organizational arrangements of the firm, but also the structure of the product market is partly dependent on the firm's organizational structure. This implies that, even if in a given industry a particular form, the M-form for instance, is identified as the socially optimal mode of organization of activities, a different, more costly structure could prevail as a result of the search for monopoly profits. The enterprise may decide not to minimize transaction costs because additional costs would enable it to exploit inefficiency in external allocation of resources in a way that results in net profit. This approach is based on the strategic conception of relations between economic agents and environment: In the same way that market structures are not totally exogenous and are partially manipulated by players, organizational structures form a decision variable allowing the setup and reinforcement of a system of market control. In a framework in which institutions and rules are explained by their functional role, the possibility that certain organizational forms adopted in equilibrium do not correspond to minimization of transaction costs is not the outcome of nonmaximization (or of x-inefficiency in the sense of Leibenstein (1983)) but results instead from a dominant strategy that does not assume as a given the actions of other economic agents.[14] If it is useful to deal with efficiency in organizational structure and not simply in production processes, it is equally important to deal with strategic behavior at both these levels.

There are many ways in which a firm can obtain monopoly rent by adopting organizational structures that restrict its rivals' choices. Some of the more well-known methods are the setup of a cartel agreement and its stabilization through various expenditures,[15] the modification of property rights through a merger,[16] and the establishment of a series of controls on a whole network of firms through interlinked shareholding[17] and interlocking directorship. For all these various instruments one can imagine situations in which a simple contract between suppliers and distributors would have realized, for example, the proposed transaction at minimum cost; but these same situations would have the firm resort to a more costly form, for instance, a legal merger or controlling shareholding, in order to set up a barrier vis-à-vis existing rivals or potential entrants. Or indeed a firm could adopt a highly decentralized multidivisional organization, but the concern about the use of one of its products as a strategic instrument in order to build a dominant position for its other activities or about the creation of a zone of influence would lead the general directorate to manage this particular production in a much more centralized fashion and to use in this case a U-form.[18] In the same way a joint venture, between a multinational and local partners would be justified in its concern to gain rapid control of the local market or to limit risks of such an entry, even if this poses problems in terms of the retention of internal control over operations. Many other institutional examples should be considered. Thus the imposition of collective bargaining of wages at the industry level can increase the costs of labor-intensive firms more than the costs of large capital-intensive firms (Williamson 1968). In an imperfect capital market the establishment of privileged financial connections with private or public credit institutions generates a capacity for resistance that does not necessarily depend on higher efficiency. Entering into long-term agreements with the state, opening to public shareholding, or resorting to various instruments of "concerted economy" may ensure discrimination with respect to competitors and entrants and may favor attainment of changes in technical norms, health regulations affecting products, rules of granting public credits or subsidies, and fiscal legislation or legislation regarding access to the profession.

In mixed economies some large industrial groups are indeed capable of controlling, up to a certain point, their legal and institutional environment, not because of superior efficiency but because of their bargaining power arising from the absolute weight that they represent in the whole of the economy, particularly with regard to employment.

On the basis of the remarks developed in section 4.4, let me emphasize that these investments in organizational and institutional structures create highly credible threats as a result of their obvious sunk cost character and their extreme specificity. The general consequence of these investments is the increase in rivals' costs. This increase is itself linked with additional expenditure for the firm using this strategy, but the investment is often made profitable more easily than the use of price competition.

Figure 5.4 illustrates this argument. Consider an industry composed of a dominant firm, benefiting from cost advantage and acting as price leader, and a competitive fringe producing a quantity at which price equals marginal cost. On the left-hand side of the figure, the supply curve of the fringe is assumed to be the marginal cost curve of a "representative firm." Besides its price policy, the dominant firm is assumed to hold a second strategic variable, namely, the option to adopt an organizational structure to which other firms must react; in this case, assume that a vertical integration that can increase input prices for producers in the fringe is possible.[19] Let D, O_{f_1}, D_{d_1}, and CM_{d_1} be the demand facing the industry, the initial supply of the fringe, the initial residual demand facing the dominant firm, and the initial average cost of this firm, respectively.

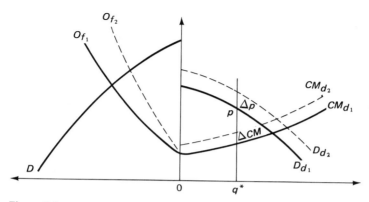

Figure 5.4
Vertical integration as a strategy of a dominant firm.

At the equilibrium industrial configuration, the dominant firm (right-hand side of figure 5.4) produces q^*, and its profits are $(p - CM_{d_1})q^*$. After vertical integration the marginal cost curve of the fringe shifts upward, reducing the fringe's supply at all prices. The residual demand facing the dominant firm D_{d_2} is increased as a result. This increase depends on the increase in marginal costs of the fringe and is weighted by market demand elasticity: The more inelastic the demand, the more the residual demand will go up (because the supply by the fringe has been reduced). The profitability of such an integration strategy for the dominant firm is determined by a comparison of the increase in price with the increase in its average cost: A sufficient condition is that the change in residual demand Δp be greater than the increase in average cost ΔCM at the initial output level q^*.[20]

A slightly different type of approach is likely to shed some light on the roles of monopoly power and cost minimization in the choice of an organizational structure (see Boyer and Jacquemin (1985)).

In the framework of the model of the dominant firm, assume that the dominant firm has the option of realizing a vertical integration that enables it to control a strategic input and thus to increase its rivals' costs. The strategic modification of the firm's organizational form is associated with an increase in its fixed costs, arising from the expenses necessary to carry out the merger (or for taking a controlling share) and the resulting reorganization; on the other hand, the modification can lead to an increase in the firm's monopoly power, because of the price increase, which for a given level of output follows the decrease in production of the competitive fringe. The problem, therefore, is to formulate the model so that it takes into account the dependence of the degree of monopoly not only on demand (and on marginal cost c, assumed constant here) but also on fixed costs.

Define $r(q)$ as the inverse of residual demand $q(p) = f(p) - \phi(p)$ facing the dominant firm, where $f(p)$ is the total demand and $\phi(p)$ is the supply of the fringe. Let $L = (p - c)/p$ be the degree of monopoly of the dominant firm, and let F be its fixed expenditure associated with organizational strategies. The problem then is to maximize

$$\max_{L,F,q} \pi(L, F, q) = Lr(q)q - F \tag{5.1}$$

subject to $g(L, F, q) = 0$. Equation (5.1) suggests that a given level of profits can be defined for a given level of output q by different combinations of the degree of monopoly L and of fixed costs F and that for a given level of sales net profits can be increased either by a rise in the degree of monopoly or a reduction in fixed costs.

Although the degree of monopoly is not dependent on F in equation (5.1), it is related to it through the constraint $g(L, F, q) = 0$.[21] This relationship says that the choices of the dominant firm, that is, its output level, its fixed costs of organization, and its degree of monopoly, must be realizable. Output level q can be increased if L is reduced and/or if F is increased; L is reduced when the firm accepts a lower rate of margin, in this case a lower price; F increases as a result of strategic vertical integration, which is reflected by better control of the input market and by an increase in L.

Various equilibrium relations can be drawn from the first-order conditions. For example, the elasticity of sales level $r(q)q$ with respect to the monopoly index should be equal to -1: for a dominant firm that has maximized profits, a 10% increase in the rate of margin L should lead to a 10% decrease in its sales.

This kind of step is still embryonic, and the study of organizational forms as instruments of market domination is far from developed. In a way, it is a "missing link" in the analysis of industrial organization. This is what the matrix presented in figure 5.5 suggests. The matrix is also a convenient way of presenting a synthesis of the arguments developed up to this point. It contains four subsets: Actions can be carried out at two levels, production and organization, and can belong to two types, search for efficiency and search for strategic commitment. The concept of efficiency refers here to cost minimization for a given activity level, whereas strategic behavior corre-

Level \ Type	Efficiency (E)	Strategy (S)
Production (P)	Efficiency in production (EP)	Strategy in production (SP)
Organization (O)	Efficiency in organization (EO)	Strategy in organization (SO)

Figure 5.5
Four basic types of corporate action analyzed in industrial organization.

sponds to expenditures that modify the conditions of action of actual or potential rivals. The notion that I put forward through this matrix is that the existence, predominance, and persistence of large firms or industrial groups is explained by a model in which the groups maximize profits by adopting actions based simultaneously on these four subsets (EP, SP, EO, SO).

Most studies of industrial organizations have been carried out at the level of production (P). The large industrial firm has been explained both by the necessity to realize economies of scale and of scope (EP) and by the will to erect barriers to entry and to mobility by manipulating conditions of production and sale (SP). As we have seen, there are also important articles in the literature devoted to the justification of the emergence of large enterprises on the basis of the search for internal efficiency in terms of transaction costs (EO). The link between the study of organizational forms on the one hand and strategic competition and credible threats on the other corresponds to the subset SO.[22]

For those who consider that "what exists is reasonably efficient," the firms' behavior can be summarized as in column E of figure 5.5. In this context all observed industrial configurations—competitive, oligopolistic, or monopolistic—are assumed to correspond to a stationary equilibrium realizing an optimum. According to this logic even the behavior classified in the second column (S) can be qualified as strategic only in a static model or in a dynamic model with perfect information. But, in fact, these actions would belong to column E if placed in a relevant model, that is, a dynamic model with incomplete information. For example, the development of faithfulness to a brand through specific advertising investment might appear to be a barrier to entry, given its largely irreversible and sunk nature. Nevertheless these activities could have some value to consumers: They wish to be tied to the incumbent because information is scarce and costly. More fundamentally, this alleged barrier would be a characteristic of an optimal allocation when incomplete information has been incorporated. In general, once the role of externalities, incomplete information, and various market failures have been taken into account, it is preferable to consider so-called strategic actions as the least objectionable response to friction typical of the real world (Demsetz 1982; de Allesi 1983).

> Existing firms have an advantage only insofar as their existence commands loyalty. Existence commands loyalty only if it reflects lower real cost of transacting, industry specific investments, or a reputable history, as, in general, it will. A reputable history is an asset to the firm possessing it and to the buyer who relies on it because information is not free. (Demsetz 1982, pp. 50–51)

On the other hand, those who place the emphasis on column S of the matrix believe that the firm responds in a strategic manner to environmental pressures, partly by amplifying the imperfections of this environment at the expense of rivals and consumers. In a dynamic framework with incomplete information, the firm can create or modify structures over time, manipulate information by investing in "disinformation," and alter the rules of the game, organizational forms, and institutions to its own advantage. There is then no presumption that such strategic behavior is socially efficient, even as a second best solution (Marris and Mueller 1980).

The most realistic approach is probably to recognize that the firm, in its search for profitable activities, resorts to the whole possible array of actions. The proportion of firms governed by efficiency considerations compared with those aiming to control markets will vary over time for a given industry and, at a given moment of time, will vary from one industry to the other.[23] In order to avoid an ex post rationalization of all types of firm behavior in terms of either efficiency or market power, one should then try to specify ex ante the constraints and the existing alternatives.[24]

Notes

1. See, in particular, the studies of Coase (1937), Hayek (1945), Arrow (1974), and Spence (1975).

2. An important difference between the approach adopted by Alchian and Demsetz and the one used by Williamson is that for Alchian and Demsetz the necessity of organization stems from the technological advantange of realizing production as a team coupled with the impossibility of identifying the marginal product of each member of the team (rewards accrue to the team, not to the individual members). This organization should then allow the establishment of individual inducements compatible with this mode of joint production and avoid a costly resort to a multitude of bilateral exchanges. For Williamson the problem of information does not result from technological conditions of team production but from economic agents' own characteristics, such as opportunistic behavior and limited rationality.

3. The ideal type is a limiting concept corresponding to a "rational utopia," in which some characteristic features of reality are chosen and accentuated so that their implications can be better elucidated and their contrasts better highlighted. Reality generally corresponds to various overlaps and combinations of ideal types. See Weber (1965).

4. The problems of overcoming divergence of interests between "principals and agents" in an uncertain environment and of elaborating appropriate managerial incentive schemes are difficult to solve, especially if it is admitted that strategic as well as informational aspects must be taken into account. Compare Nalebuff and Stiglitz (1983) and Vickers (1985).

5. See also Chandler (1977), p. 6. His analysis is further enriched in his 1982 article.

6. This is not necessarily the best. For example, high substitution costs may simply reinforce the worry to find initially a supplier

with the lowest price, which would subsequently reduce the temptation to change. Von Weizsacker (1984) has analyzed the compatibility of the existence of such costs with long-term competition. By contrast, Klemperer (1984) constructed a model in which higher switching costs can promote collusive behavior.

7. There exists an obvious link between economies of scale and economies of scope: For example, an indivisible asset may be the basis of economies of scope if it serves as input for many production processes. For an analysis of this link, see Baumol et al. (1982), ch. 3.

8. Note that the M-form is less appropriate if operational divisions cannot be completely segmented and if they display a non-negligible degree of interdependence at the technological or market level. Interdivisional connections are then necessary. Moreover, the problem of functional interfaces is not resolved.

9. In this case a firm situated downstream owns tools and specialized equipment used by firms upstream who manufacture parts for the product range. A typical example is that of car assembly firms, who own the specialized tools used by their suppliers in manufacturing car parts. So long as the firm downstream holds contractual relations with its suppliers, the merger is not complete.

10. See studies by Imai and Itami (1984) and Goto (1982), which throw some light on the specificity of Japanese organizational forms. For European groups, see de Woot and Desclee (1985).

11. See, for example, Arrow (1975), who studied the case in which the vertically integrated firm is able to obtain information on supply conditions before a firm that is not integrated can. For his part, Carlton (1979) argued that vertical integration is a means of transferring risk from one sector to another.

12. For the American case, see Hayes and Abernathy (1983); for the Japanese case, see Aoki (1983); and for the European case, see Geroski and Jacquemin (1984).

13. In the United States and in Europe the development of intrapreneurship and "internal business units" expresses a similar trend.

14. It must be stressed that the question here is not for a specific organizational form to choose rules of procedure and types of

inducement. The strategic choice concerns the form itself. Another related problem is that of methods that avoid conflict of objectives within the enterprise. For Alchian and Demsetz the problem does not exist: Activities inside the firm are regulated, as are external activities, through different types of contracts, assumed to have been drawn freely. Hence questions of authority, power, and constraint disappear. For Williamson the problem is there but is essentially the same as the elaboration of hierarchical structures that avoid distortions with respect to the sole objectives of the general directorate. Finally, the *theory of the agent and the principal* concerns the expenses needed to prevent the delegation of authority from leading to a divergence between the behavior of the agent and the interests of the principal (see, in particular, the special issue of the *Journal of Law and Economics,* June 1983). These are unilateral approaches that ignore many aspects of the abuse of power in the enterprise.

15. In their study of the history of rationing agreements relating to the production of crude oil, Libecap and Wiggings (1984) showed that, although these arrangements prevent the minimization of production costs, they are "efficient" means of limiting the dissipation of monopoly rent. Libecap and Wiggings also highlighted the positive role played by a high degree of concentration in bringing about these accords.

16. Paroush and Peles (1981) have built an interesting model in which firms producing separately and efficiently the components of a certain range are nevertheless led to merge in order to extract more of the consumer surplus. For vertical integration, see Perry (1978).

17. Given limited initial capital, the system of interlinked majority shareholding allows the control of considerable total assets through a multiplier effect. Let A_r be the productive asset of firm r, and let B_r be the degree of control exerted by firm $r - 1$ (upstream) on firm r $(r = 1, \ldots, n)$, where $B_r > 50\%$, $r > 0$; B_0 is the share of the majority shareholder in the initial mother company. This shareholder holds only $\Sigma_{r=0}^{n} A_r (\Pi_0^r B_k)$ but controls $\Sigma_{r=0}^{n} A_r$. The multiplier effect m is therefore easily defined as

$$m = \sum_{r=0}^{n} A_r \bigg/ \sum_{r=0}^{n} A_r \left(\prod_0^r B_k \right).$$

18. See Pinardon and Ponssard (1983) for case studies.

19. There have been many discussions on the conditions under which an upstream integration with a firm holding monopoly power is a means of raising the prices of the final product. Such conditions may exist when technology does not impose fixed proportions and when constant returns to scale are absent.

20. It is clear that, in general, the dominant firm will increase its profits even further by adjusting its output. For the corresponding model, see Salop and Scheffman (1983).

21. Assuming that the constraint $g(L, F, q) = 0$ can be written explicitly as $L = L(F, q)$, we can rewrite the general problem in a more simple way:

$$\max_{q, F} L(F, q)r(q)q - F.$$

The appropriate concavity conditions are assumed to be satisfied.

22. It would be useful to analyze all the links existing between the four subsets. For example, one aspect of the link between EP and EO is that internalization could be preferred to the price system, despite important agency difficulties and opportunistic behavior, because these difficulties are more than compensated for by economies of scale or of scope.

23. For an econometric study of French industrial groups which suggests that according to the type of industry the presence of these groups can be explained by the pursuit of either technological efficiency or monopoly power, see Encaoua and Jacquemin (1982).

24. General remarks on this theme are made in Elster (1979) and van Parys (1981).

References

A. Alchian and H. Demsetz. 1972. "Production, information costs and economic organization." *American Economic Review* 62(5):777–795.

M. Aoki. 1983. "Managerialism revisited in the light of bargaining-game theory." *International Journal of Industrial Organization* 1:1–21.

M. Aoki. 1984. "Innovative adaptation through the quasi-tree structure: An emerging aspect of Japanese entrepreneurship." *Zeitschrift für Nationalökonomie* 4:25–35.

K. Arrow. 1974. *Limits of Organization.* Amsterdam: North-Holland.

K. Arrow. 1975. "Vertical integration and communication." *Bell Journal of Economics* 1:173–183.

W. Baumol, J. Panzar, and R. Willig. 1982. *Contestable Markets and the Theory of Industry Structure.* New York: Harcourt Brace Jovanovich.

M. Boyer and A. Jacquemin. 1985. "Organizational choices for efficiency and market power." *Economics Letters* 1:79–82.

D. Carlton. 1979. "Vertical integration in competitive markets under uncertainty." *Journal of Industrial Economics* 3:189–209.

A. Chandler. 1977. *The Visible Hand: The Managerial Revolution in American Business.* Cambridge: Harvard University Press.

A. Chandler. 1982. "The M-form: Industrial groups American style." *European Economic Review* 19:3–23.

R. Coase. 1937. "The nature of the firm." *Economica* 4:386–405.

H. Daems. 1980. "The determinants of the hierarchical organization of industry." Working paper 80-18, European Institute for Advanced Studies in Management.

H. Demsetz. 1982. "Barriers to entry." *American Economic Review* 72(1):47–57.

P. de Woot and X. Desclee de Maredsous. 1985. *Le management stratégique des groupes industriels* (The strategic management of industrial groups). Paris: Cabay-Economica.

L. de Allesi. 1983. "Property rights, transaction costs and x-efficiency." *American Economic Review* 73(1):64–81.

J. Elster. 1979. *Ulysses and the Sirens.* Paris: Edition de la Maison des Sciences de l'Homme.

D. Encaoua and A. Jacquemin. 1982. "Organizational efficiency and monopoly power: The case of French industrial groups." *European Economic Review* 19:25–51.

P. Geroski and A. Jacquemin. 1984. "Large firms in the European corporate economy and industrial policy in the '80s," in *European Industry: Public Policy and Corporate Strategy*, A. Jacquemin (ed.). Oxford: Oxford University Press, 343–367.

A. Goto. 1982. "Business groups in a market economy." *European Economic Review* 19:53–70.

F. Hayek. 1945. "The use of knowledge in society." *American Economic Review* 35:519–530.

R. Hayes and B. Abernathy. 1983. "Managing our way to economic decline," in *Survival Strategies of American Industry*, Harvard Business Review (ed.). New York: Wiley, 15–35.

K. Imai and H. Itami. 1984. "Interpenetration of organization and market." *International Journal of Industrial Organization* 2:285–310.

P. Klemperer. 1984. "Collusion via switching costs." Discussion paper 786, Stanford University Graduate School of Business.

H. Leibenstein. 1983. "Property rights and x-efficiency: Comment." *American Economic Review* 4:831–842.

G. Libecap and S. Wiggings. 1984. "Contractual responses to the common pool." *American Economic Review* 74(1):87–98.

R. Marris and D. Mueller. 1980. "The corporation and competition." *Journal of Economic Literature* 18:32–63.

J. Marschak and R. Radner. 1972. *Economic Theory of Teams*. New Haven: Yale University Press.

B. Nalebuff and J. Stiglitz. 1983. "Information, competition, and markets." *American Economic Review* 73(2):278–283.

J. Panzar and R. Willig. 1975. "Economies of scale and economies of scope in multioutput production." Bell Labs Economic Discussion Paper 33.

J. Paroush and Y. Peles. 1981. "A combined monopoly and optimal packaging." *European Economic Review* 15:373–383.

M. Perry. 1978. "Price discrimination and forward integration." *Bell Journal of Economics* 9:209–217.

F. Pinardon and J. P. Ponssard. 1983. "Strategic groups and industry evolution." Paper presented at the third annual conference of the Strategic Management Society, Paris.

J. P. Ponssard. 1984. "Stratégies industrielles: une synthèse fondée sur la notion de groupe stratégique" (Industrial strategies: A synthesis based on the notion of the strategic group). Laboratoire d'Economie Statistique et Gestion, ENSAE, Paris (unpublished).

S. Salop and D. Scheffman. 1983. "Raising rivals' costs." *American Economic Review* 73(2):267–271.

M. Spence. 1975. "The economics of internal organization: An introduction." *Bell Journal of Economics* 6:163–172.

D. Teece. 1980. "Economies of scope and the scope of the enterprise." *Journal of Economic Behaviour and Organization* 1:223–247.

P. Van Parys. 1981. *Evolutionary Explanation in the Social Sciences.* London: Tavistock.

J. Vickers. 1985. "Delegation and the theory of the firm." *Economic Journal,* June, supplement, 138–147.

C. von Weizsacker. 1984. "The costs of substitution." *Econometrica* 52(5):1085–1116.

M. Weber. 1965. *Essais sur la théorie de la science* (Essays on the theory of science). Paris: Flammarion.

O. Williamson. 1968. "Wage rates as a barrier to entry." *Quarterly Journal of Economics* 82(1):85–116.

O. Williamson. 1971. "Managerial discretion, organizational form and the multidivision hypothesis," in *The Corporate Economy,* R. Marris and A. Wood (eds.). London: Macmillan, 343–386.

O. Williamson. 1975. *Markets and Hierarchies: Analysis and Antitrust Implications.* New York: Free Press.

O. Williamson. 1981. "The modern corporation: Origins, evolution, attributes." *Journal of Economic Literature* 19:1537–1568.

O. Williamson and W. Ouchi. 1983. "The markets and hierarchies programmes of research: Origins, implications, prospects," in *Power, Efficiency and Institution: A Critical Appraisal of the "Markets and Hierarchies Paradigm,"* D. Francis, J. Turk, and P. Willman (eds.). London: Heinemann, 85–125.

R. Wilson. 1975. "Informational economies of scale." *Bell Journal of Economics* 6:184–195.

6   Industrial Policy and Models of Society

In the previous chapters recent theoretical research in industrial organization was used to establish a contrast between studies that emphasize efficiency of selection through market mechanisms and those that shed light on the role of strategic behavior (private or public) affecting these same mechanisms. It is clear that the roles attributed to economic policy in general and to industrial policy in particular will be different according to the weight given to these two paradigms. I discuss this in section 6.1.

Beyond our economic policy problem, the choice of a model of industrial society is at stake. In the eyes of many it is economic and social selection based on free competition that sorts out the fittest individuals and organizations. A radical expression of this view is to consider that economics, law, and political science are all destined to become branches of "sociobiology," whose task it is to explain all social behavior on the basis of natural selective processes. Section 6.2 is devoted to these developments. Finally, in section 6.3 I critically review the economic and social implications of these studies and put forward alternative perspectives.

6.1 Market Mechanisms and Industrial Policy

Within the existing mixed economies we are not faced with a dichotomous choice between an exclusive use of market mechanism and systematic control of industrial development. On the contrary, the situation is that of a continuum in the degree of intervention: According to the branch of activity or the product and according to their phase of development, there coexist measures in all European states (including the German Federal Republic) aimed at assisting private initiative, restructuring or liquidating certain activities, and finally taking direct charge of certain industrial projects.

On the other hand, at the theoretical level there is an everlasting debate between those for whom industrial policy should be rejected and those who wish to give it a positive role. In this section I would like to review these arguments briefly in the light of my previous discussions.

For those who have full confidence in market mechanisms, the only real requirement is the existence of a healthy macroeconomic environment. All industrial policy must be either excluded or simply a general label for all measures aimed at facilitating an automatic process of industrial adjustment: A good infrastructure, a professionally adapted labor force, easy access to capital and credit, and a fiscal policy unopposed to economic rationality are all conditions that must be satisfied in order for the price system to send out the correct signals and for economic agents to react to them correctly. In such a context it is then assumed that the market's selective game and the spontaneous forces of competition are sufficient to ensure a Pareto-efficient equilibrium. In fact, any form of industrial policy is not viewed with favor. On the one hand, policies aimed at slowing down the process of structural change or keeping alive declining sectors must be rejected:[1]

The damage to the rest of the economy is greater the longer a stricken industry is allowed to prolong the agony and secondly, it is not obvious that prolonged adjustment is really any easier to bear than quick surgery. (Curzon-Price 1981, p. 120)

On the other hand, "positive" industrial policies that are meant to accelerate structural mutations are equally condemned. To start with, the government, failing an adequate criterion, is unable to determine which industries are to be promoted, and, besides, this kind of interference leads to a system in which economic decisions are politicized and freedom of initiative is stifled.

In contrast, there is a whole tide of research questioning whether the market alone can efficiently accomplish selections leading to new industrial organizations. Once we reject the idea that industrial policy is simply another name for protectionism, we can distinguish two levels of argument.

First, we can refer to the long list of so-called market "failures": the existence of important externalities, many products and resources having the character of public goods, the role of strong indivisibilities linked with nonconvexities in production and organization, and consequences of uncertainty in an economy in which all intertemporal and all contingent markets do not exist so that some mutually advantageous exchanges between agents are prevented. Public authorities could then favor organizational forms that internalize the external effects of important technological choices and promote the emergence of poles of competition; through financial aids and specific public programs they would be required to support research and development in high technology industries (microcomputers, aerospace, biotechnology) affected by important fixed and sunk costs; they should ensure a minimum socialization of risks in activities characterized by high levels of risks and incomplete information. Macroeconomic policy alone is insufficient to deal with this kind of problem and may even create perverse effects despite its apparent "neutrality." If it is accepted that inter- and intra-industrial variations are significant and that the degree of price flexibility depends in particular on structural characteristics of each industry, then macroeconomic measures without microeconomic foundations are likely to be incompatible with the adjustment process occurring in real markets. A recent empirical study of many countries by the Organization for Economic Cooperation and Development (OECD) shows that different industrial categories do indeed behave differently so far as their price flexibility over time is concerned and that well-defined structural variables have a systematic effect on these categories.[2] Hence it appears necessary to be aware of these characteristics of the productive system in order to be able to predict the effects of macroeconomic policies and to complement them by less aggregated and more specific actions. Compatibility between macroeconomic constraints and industrial behavior is not automatic.

A second level of argument in favor of a positive industrial policy goes beyond the consideration of failures inherent in certain markets. It concerns strategies that deliberately influence the transformation and the industrial reorganization of sectors, and nations. Although the traditional theory of international trade is based on the competitive model and assumes factor endowments to be "natural" and exogenous, it is maintained that in many sectors comparative advantages are based on partially controllable elements. For instance, public policies may alter the process of accumulation of physical and human capital over time, and the outcome of these accumulated investments would in turn modify relative capital endowments.

Japanese industrial policy is the best known case. Over

fifteen years ago, Ojimi, minister at the time, made the following declaration:

> The MITI [Ministry of International Trade and Industry] decided to establish in Japan industries which require intensive employment of capital and technology, industries that in consideration of comparative cost of production should be the most inappropriate for Japan, industries such as steel, oil-refining, petrochemicals, automobiles, aircraft, industrial machinery of all sorts, and electronics, including electronic computers. From a short-run, static viewpoint, encouragement of such industries would seem to conflict with economic rationalism. But, from a long-range viewpoint, these are precisely the industries where income elasticity of demand is high, technological progress is rapid, and labor productivity rises fast. It was clear that without these industries it would be difficult to employ a population of 100 million and raise their standard of living to that of Europe and America with light industries alone. . . . According to Napoleon and Clausewitz, the secret of a successful strategy is the concentration of fighting power on the main battleground; fortunately, owing to good luck and wisdom spawned by necessity, Japan has been able to concentrate its scant capital in strategic industries. (OECD, 1972, p. 149)

Even if some authors believe that Japanese consumers have suffered significant implicit costs to ensure such a development, they agree[3] that the industrial policy of Japan, based on national consensus and a close relation between firms and the government, has been successful and has made a substantial contribution to the increase in Japan's real income. Undoubtedly, the Japanese sociocultural model cannot be transposed to the European context, and its future is uncertain. Nevertheless the experience of Japan has shown the usefulness of a strategic approach to industrial problems and the existence of novel forms of organization and allocation of resources that have proved efficient, even though they are quite different from those preached in our countries.[4]

Today, a growing number of models based on various policy instruments offer an analytical basis for such a strategic approach. The common idea is that, in the dynamic context of imperfect competition and international trade, policy intervention can improve welfare by influencing equilibrium outcomes within given rules of the game (for example, by shifting a Cournot-Nash equilibrium) or by changing the rules themselves (for example, by creating a first-mover advantage so that the solution concept is no longer Cournot). It can be argued that a government can sometimes do so more ably than private agents because of its higher degree of credibility based on its reputation and/ or resources or because of the expected inertia of policies, once adopted.

In what follows I present two theoretical examples in which there are interactions between two governments. In the first case there is a conflict between the two national welfares, and in the second situation the strategic action by one government improves welfare for both.[5]

For the first case, assume an economy composed of two countries having the same potential demand for a new high technology product. This demand is assumed to be linear in each country: $q_1 = 6 - p_1$ and $q_2 = 6 - p_2$, where p is price per unit of product. If there are no barriers to international trade, world demand is $q_1 + q_2 = 12 - 2p$, with $p = p_1 = p_2$. Assume that there are two firms, one per country, and that each can realize the new product at a fixed cost, for example, a sunk cost in research and development of $F = 7$. Once this investment has been made, production takes place at zero cost. If the two firms decide to enter into this type of activity, they will find themselves in a duopoly situation and thus are assumed to have Cournot-type behavior. In this case the profit function of firm 1 is

$$\pi_1 = p(q_1, q_2)q_1 - F = 6q_1 - 0.5q_1^2 - 0.5q_1q_2 - F,$$

given that $p = 6 - (q_1 + q_2)/2$. First-order conditions imply that in equilibrium

$$q_1^* = 6 - 0.5q_2.$$

Similarly, for firm 2 we get

$$q_2^* = 6 - 0.5q_1.$$

Hence at Cournot equilibrium each firm sells a quantity of 4, applies a price of 2, and realizes a profit of 1. In country 1 the consumer surplus is

$$s = \int_0^{q_1} p\,dq_1 - pq_1 = \int_0^4 (6 - q_1)dq_1 - pq_1 = 8.$$

Therefore the sum of consumers' and producers' surplus in this country is equal to 9.

Table 6.1 helps to analyze the decision of whether or not to enter in the new technological activity, that is, whether or not to produce the new product. Two situations are distinguished: one in which there is free trade between the two countries and one in which public authorities of country 1 have set up a credible barrier preventing entry of the product of firm 2 into their territory. The three values in parentheses show the consumer surplus of country 1, the profit of firm 1, and the profit of firm 2, respectively. On the basis of the parameters adopted in the example, both firms find it profitable to enter, in the case of free ex-

Table 6.1
Import protection as export promotion

Choice of firm 1	Choice of firm 2			
	Free trade		Market 1 protected	
	To enter	Not to enter	To enter	Not to enter
To enter	(8, 1, 1)	(4.5, 11, 0)	(4.5, 6, −3)	(4.5, 11, 0)
Not to enter	(4.5, 0, 11)	(0, 0, 0)	(0, 0, 1)	(0, 0, 0)

change. And once the Cournot equilibrium has been achieved, there is no credible threat that the private agents can use to modify this equilibrium.

If on the other hand, the government of country 1 commits itself irreversibly to protect its market, the situation is different. Firm 1 will then have monopoly in country 1, and there will be duopoly in market 2. Firm 1 will have a turnover of 3×3 \$ in market 1 and 2×2 \$ in market 2, making a net profit of 6. But in fact, as the table indicates, firm 2 would in this case have a turnover of 2×2 and therefore a loss of -3. Hence firm 2 will not enter, abandoning the totality of the market to firm 1. The total surplus of producers and consumers in country 1 will then be equal to 15.5, which is higher than the level obtained in a situation of free trade. The crucial point is that import restrictions allow the protected firm to control not only its domestic market but also the foreign market: Protection against imports is transformed into promotion of exports! The asymmetry between the two governments and the existence of significant fixed costs entailed by the production of the new product play an essential role here.

In the second example,[6] we consider a game between the United States and the European Economic Community governments in a world in which the incumbent firm is American, and there is a potential EEC entrant firm. The US incumbent has sunk costs K that have already been incurred. In the US market, let PU_1 = excess of revenue over production cost for a monopolist; PU_2 = excess of revenue over production cost for each duopolist; SU_1 = consumers' surplus under monopoly; and SU_2 = consumers' surplus under duopoly. Define PE_1, PE_2, SE_1, and SE_2 analogously for the EEC market. The problem is the following. The two governments have to choose between free trade and complete protection, which bans all imports; the EEC government has to decide whether to subsidize the

EEC entrant's sunk costs, the part of its production costs that corresponds to the costs already sunk by the US incumbent; and the EEC firm has to decide whether or not it wishes to enter.

Given perfect information, we can calculate the solution as follows: First, calculate optimal actions in the second-stage game; then calculate optimal actions in the prior first-stage game. A taxonomy of possible outcomes is discussed in Dixit and Kyle (1985). For my illustrative purpose I focus on the post-entry trade policy game. For simplicity I take marginal costs as constant and assume away any international reselling. Table 6.2 shows the payoffs of different government actions. An outcome labeled $(A; B)$ implies that the payoff to the United States is A and to the European community B. For $SU_2 + PU_2 > SU_1 + PU_1$, the US government prefers free trade no matter which policy the EEC government selects. Similarly, if $SE_2 + PE_2 > SE_1 + PE_1$, the EEC government prefers free trade no matter which policy the US government selects. Hence free trade will be chosen, and the EEC entrant knows this in advance in deciding whether or not to enter. Entry is then profitable for the EEC firm if $PE_2 + PU_2 - K$ is positive, but for an industry with large sunk costs K, this expression will be negative, and entry will not take place. If the EEC government is allowed to move first, it could have an interest in making an irreversible precommitment. By paying the EEC firm's sunk cost K, the EEC government can ensure that

Table 6.2
Post-entry trade policy game

	EEC protection	EEC free trade
US protection	$(SU_1 + PU_1;$ $SE_1 + PE_1 - K)$	$(SU_1 + PU_1 + PE_2;$ $SE_2 + PE_2 - K)$
US free trade	$(SU_2 + PU_2;$ $SE_1 + PE_1 + PU_2 - K)$	$(SU_2 + PU_2 + PE_2;$ $SE_2 + PE_2 + PU_2 - K)$

the final equilibrium will be free trade with a duopoly, which yields not only greater benefits to the Europeans than the alternative policy of complete protection but also greater benefits to the United States than the alternative of protection by the EEC. More generally, Dixit and Kyle concluded that the inability of firms to appropriate all consumers' surplus can sometimes justify a public policy to alter oligopolistic market oucomes, even from the viewpoint of worldwide efficiency.

A good practical illustration of industrial policy as strategic behavior at the international level is the public support offered to the European Airbus Consortium in its efforts to challenge the incumbent (Boeing) in the market for intermediate-range commercial airliners. A deal with Pan Am marked a further consolidation of the Airbus foothold in this market and surpassed earlier sales in domestic European or third markets. The success of Airbus to date is not derived solely from European cooperation in pooling knowledge, thus placing Airbus on a par with the United States, where the award of grants and research and development contracts through an open bid system results (particularly in the aerospace industry) in a common pool of knowledge. The collective governmental precommitment to Airbus also raised Boeing's cost of trying to fight off the entry challenge and thereby increased the chance of successful entry. Still, the relative positions in the future are an open question.

It is interesting to contrast this case with the semiconductor industry, in which, until now, Europe has been unable to challenge the first movers. It is well known that European firms in this industry have lagged international rivals, especially in integrated circuits (OECD, 1985). Three factors can explain the situation.

A major factor is the early presence in Europe of subsidiaries of US corporations whose mother companies developed with the help of a large domestic market, with its great public demand for new and sophisticated military devices (a form of industrial policy!). This market supported the production of most new semiconductor devices several years before the European (and Japanese) markets. By the time sufficient demand arose in Europe to support local production, new European firms were already at a competitive disadvantage relative to American subsidiaries, which enjoyed licensing and technical assistance agreements with their mother companies. It is also interesting to note that the foreign subsidiaries that diffused new technology in Europe were not old foreign subsidiaries, such as ITT, but new ones set up mainly in the 1960s. Thus Tilton (1972, p. 165) concludes:

These firms manage to evade the entry barriers blocking new domestic firms because their parent companies share with them much of the know-how derived from past production experience, provide specialists and other professional personnel, and if necessary supply venture capital.

Other elements complemented the advantages of first movers in the semiconductor industry. Although the basic discoveries have diffused quickly, product development and process engineering of semiconductor technology have diffused much more slowly. Hence the acquisition of a patent or license does not effectively enable the acquirer to capture the main benefit from disembodied advances in technical knowledge. Customer-supplier relationships are also important in semiconductor and electronics subassembly process innovation, as is the necessity of working extensively with the customer after the product is introduced. Thus the existing relationships betwen US subsidiaries and their buyers may have operated as an important aspect of product differentiation barriers to entry. Moreover, there is a requirement for specialized facilities and specific production and marketing skills. It takes time for entrants to acquire these, and this has two implications. First, firms that use semiconductor process equipment to make semiconductors for end-use will face significant barriers in trying to move into the production of semiconductor process equipment itself, barriers that arise from the high degree of specificity of know-how, organization arrangements, and production infrastructure. Second, incumbents have important first-mover advantages once they are established with one strong product in which their costs are largely sunk, on the back of which they can continue to widen and extend their product range (Coughlan and Flaherty 1983).

A further set of problems has arisen from the characteristics of European policies toward semiconductors. Within each country, few government research and development and production contracts were awarded to new firms trying to enter the semiconductor industry, as this was deemed likely to divert support from the few large firms chosen as national champions to develop viable alternatives to American subsidiaries. This procurement policy raised the barriers to entry in these countries, making it difficult for entrants to pioneer the use of new semiconductor technology. In fact, the number of new European firms entering the industry has been small (particularly relative to the multitude of new American firms). What is worse in individual European countries is that each government has promoted its own national champion in semiconductors, thereby creating barriers that prevent genuine specialization at the European level. US and Japanese companies have been able to make a series of bilateral agreements with firms in each of the European countries, thereby preventing the emergence of serious European competition and reducing much of the European industry to the role of licensing and second-sourcing US and Japanese technology.

These factors lead to the possibility of a concerted European industrial policy that will help overcome industry strategies along national lines,[7] reduce barriers between national champions, and develop a large home European market for industrial applications.

The idea behind the airline and semiconductor industry illustrations was not to examine the content of industrial policies as they are envisaged or put into practice in Europe, the United States, or Japan. Studies on this theme are numerous.[8] Rather the aim was to show the specific roles that public players can assume in the unfolding of strategic games. The respective weights of these players meanwhile will vary according to conceptions of our industrial societies and according to national characteristics.

From this point of view it is useful to recall the two types of correction mechanism analyzed by Hirschman (1971). In the first type, referred to as *exit*, a consumer, or more generally a member of an organization, who is not satisfied with the product offered by a firm or the service provided by an organization will leave this firm or organization in favor of another: Dissatisfaction is marked by an exit. In contrast, the second type, referred to as *voice*, is the set of all means, excluding exit, through which a consumer or a member of an organization directly expresses its dissatisfaction to those in charge, with the view of initiating internal transformation. Compared to the anonymity of the vote (retreat) by means of the market, the second kind of correction mechanism expresses itself through an utterance of grievance and the concern with modifying the performance of one's supplier or those who manage the organization to which one belongs. A priori, the voice mechanism will be preferred to the exit mechanism if the latter is inefficient in recovering incurred losses (in particular, in the case of lack of close substitutes), thus leading to the most active and lucid members leaving the firm or organization, and if clients/members have the means to make their action effective through the voice mechanism. To these factors must be added the role of *loyalty*, or the feeling of faithfulness toward a relationship or a group. Such an "affectio societatis" in fact implies that one gives up the certainty of improvement in one's position through exit, in favor of the uncertainty of improvement through voice. Loyalty, if it provides an additional or prolonged chance of recuperation and if it stops deterioration processes that are not necessarily irreversible, acts as a useful barrier to exit.

In my framework the mechanisms described by Hirschman can be interpreted as follows. In exit social change is ensured through a decentralized and anonymous mechanism that secures victory for the most efficient. Winners are awarded with growth, and losers are obliged to disappear. Results worked out by the market are considered natural and legitimate, including international, national, regional, and personal redistribution of income. In voice the process of social adjustment rests on a collective consensus that establishes solidarity of existing interests and decides the general direction of change. Consequences of change are themselves tempered by effective redistribution between winners and losers. Outcomes of market mechanisms are not automatically considered as legitimate and can be modified strategically.

A domain that is particularly useful in clarifying this comparison is that of "research and innovation." According to Ergaz (1984), American public policy in this area has been based on stimulation of the process of discovery associated with phenomena of entry and exit: The deregulation of financial markets and of important markets for the infrastructure has created new opportunities for entry in high technology industries; changes in laws regarding bankruptcy have facilitated exits; mobility of qualified workers has been encouraged; industrial standardization has facilitated exploitation of economies of scale; and strategic freedom of large firms has been increased by the shelving of antitrust laws. In contrast, European countries have increasingly turned to industrial policies aimed at guiding firms' strategies; they have limited resource mobility, especially that of labor; they have encouraged concertation between diverging interests and have made special efforts to attenuate the cost of change for the most disadvantaged.

It is clear that each of these types of correction mechanism presents grave dangers in its extreme form. In the exit type, transmitted information is poor, the mechanism is brutal, and the probability of reconciliation of conflicting social interests is low. On the contrary, there is the risk of a *dual society* developing, in which a significant proportion of the population becomes peripheral and marginalized and in which the legitimacy of the "winning circle" is as much based on a strategy of domination as on initial efficiency. In the voice type, on the other hand, the concern for consensus and equitable compensation is liable to undermine the inducement to creativity, initiative, experimentation, and diversity. Defense of group interests and acquired rights easily deviates toward corporatism and ultraconservatism.

In a universe in which natural mechanisms ensure the equivalence between equilibrium and optimum, the process of exit would be the absolute ruler, and economic policy would be reduced to possible steps toward the redistribution of income. If, on the other hand, we accept the omnipresence of strategic behavior in a more or less inevitable framework of imperfect competition, the challenge facing our societies becomes much more complex. Not only do redistributional problems become more extensive and more subtle but also inefficiencies of imperfect competition are not automatically corrected and are likely to be met with deliberate policies. These policies do not imply a growing and paralyzing interventionism on the part of public authorities but are on the contrary compatible with a severe limitation of the sphere of control of the state. To start with, one must recognize the role of the many actors and new forms of social organization that ensure, at the local, regional, national, and international levels, that options are safeguarded, that changes of suppliers are workable, and that abuses of economic power are checked. The problem therefore is not to choose between voice and exit but to combine their virtues while avoiding their vices. Nor does it boil down to a radical and irreversible choice between public initiative versus private initiative, thus freezing the abilities of each; rather it should raise the issue of the difficulty of implementing mobility in respective spheres according to appropriate modalities. For instance, deregulation of some spheres mismanaged by the state is undoubtedly desirable. This, however, does not imply the return to a utopian free market but a change of regulation: Delegation of functions, grants for public services, or transfer of assets to the private sector must be matched with institutional rules and alternative forms of social control. If the state does not act as a welfare state and renounces the monopoly of determining social welfare, it would nevertheless remain a privileged player among the participants in the games of social and economic relations. It would take on only what is strictly necessary but, in the successive disequilibria that characterize our evolution, it would safeguard pluralism, avoid replacement of public monopolies by private cartels, and ensure effective redistributive transfers.

6.2 Bioeconomy and Sociobiology

The contrasts mentioned in the previous section become more fundamental when we take into consideration recent research in sociobiology and bioeconomy. These studies not only are based on a methodology that favor selective mechanisms and adaptation to the environment but also claim to lead to a new conception of industrial and social organization.

There is nothing new in the interest shown by economists in sociobiology. According to Demsetz (1982), those who were active in the founding of the American Economic Association did not find it difficult to justify industrial concentration.

They were swept along by the tide of Darwinian thought. Combinations and trusts were regarded as evolutionary social advances, as the outcome of natural laws calling for social cooperation to replace personal actions. (p. 17).

And Demsetz concludes:

The United States is now almost two-centuries into its unique experiment to strengthen economic competition, however silly that may seem to sociobiologists. (p. 18)

For his part, Ghiselin (1978), while addressing the Association (Session on Economics and Biology) almost a century after its founding, asserted that economics and biology do not simply share common interests or provide one another with useful analogies; in fact, they constitute the same branch of knowledge.

All the properties of organisms, without exception, are the results of evolution, and the mechanism of evolution, selection, is nothing more than reproductive competition between members of the same species (p. 233)

This competition itself has a genetic basis. An organism is the vehicle of its genes[9], and evolution takes place as if the genes of living beings led to the adoption of behavior liable to ensure their optimal propagation. In his book *The Selfish Gene*, Dawkins (1976) illustrates how the gene ensures its

survival, either directly or indirectly, that is, how it behaves in a way that favors the multiplication of genes similar to its own. Individuals are therefore "survival mach-
ines" programmed for purely biological ends. As shown by
Thuillier (1981a): "Explaining a particular social behaviour
or structure becomes the same as elucidating the utility for
evolution of this behaviour or this structure" (p. 18).

Applied to economics, this vision is clearly a fundamental extension of the ideas mentioned previously that economic agents and organizations are subject to efficient
selective sorting through market mechanisms. Many recent studies have in fact made such an extension. Thus
Hirshleifer (1978) rejects the traditional economic approach
in which individual preferences are arbitrarily assumed as
given, and, using sociobiology as a base, he considers
these preferences as essentially adaptative:

Man himself, full of love and hate and sheer cussedness, ill fits
the model of "economic man"—but the gene is an "economic
gene." It has been selected to survive on the basis of successful
selfishness. . . . Depending upon opportunities, the interests of
the gene may sometimes be served if the organism housing it is
programmed to help or to hurt other organisms. (p. 240)

In a way, the old *homo economicus*, who calculated his
gains, is replaced by *homo geneticus*, who calculates his
genes! Various studies on altruism[10] (Becker 1976), division
of labor (Ghiselin 1974, 1978), and inequalities of the income distribution (Taubman 1976, 1978) have developed
from this basis. For inequalities of income distribution
there have been econometric studies to determine the per-
centage of the variance of the income distribution that can
be attributed to differences in genetic endowment.[11]

Finally, certain implications for economic policy have
been suggested. The general theme is that governmental
programs which constrain economic agents to a level of
competition and egoism that is below the level genetically

programmed are condemned to failure. "Once we can de-
rive the genetic basis for human desires," Becker[12] would
have said "we can determine which policies will work and
which will not." A typical example, according to Becker, is
family behavior. Rather than considering the family as a
homogeneous unit, devoid of any internal competition,
the family must be perceived in each of its elements. It is
then not surprising that some public policies favoring certain members at the expense of others fail. For example, it
has been shown in the United States that children of
underprivileged families who received compensatory education from such programs as Head Start, which provides
poor preschool children with preparatory programs, did
not perform better than other students belonging to the
same class but not enjoying this advantage. The explanation would be that parents who have a child in the preparatory program devote less time and money to this child
and instead put their effort into improving the genetic aptitude of their other children, thus favoring the global
chance of reproduction of these genes. For his part, Hirshleifer[13] deems, in reply to a criticism by Arrow, that the
sociobiological approach, in economics as in other fields,
leads to a deterministic view of social phenomena. To the
extent that the juridico-economic universe is largely determined by the evolutionary process, policy, be it individual
or social, is no longer relevant. On the contrary, spontaneous competitive mechanisms and laissez-faire are inevitable channels.

"Imperialism" of sociobiology is not limited to economics but applies to a whole range of disciplines, including
law and history. This final chapter is no doubt the place to
linger a moment on this issue. So far as law and institutions are concerned, two approaches can be distinguished.
For the sociobiological school law is itself a product of evolution. This view has many roots in the theories of legal

evolution.[14] One of the best known is the German historical school of jurisprudence founded by F. von Savigny, who elaborated a theory of stages of legal development. Some years later a Belgian law professor, E. Picard (1897), tried to identify the factors of such a legal evolution, including race, environment, imitation, and density of population.[15] But it has been only recently that sociobiological theories have claimed that deliberate legal constructions based on calculated "social contracts" and ignoring the "scientific" laws of evolution are useless. In his work on human nature (for which he received the Pulitzer Prize), Wilson (1978) questioned the role of philosophers, such as John Rawls and Robert Nozick, who resort to the fiction of an initial "social contract" to justify a judicial system. In his famous *Theory of Justice* (1971), Rawls begins by stating a proposition he considers beyond any discussion:

In a just society the liberties of equal citizenship are taken as settled; the rights secured by justice are not subject to political bargaining or to the calculus of social interests. (p. 5)

Nozick, for his part, sets forth just as firmly an initial proposition in his work *Anarchy, State and Utopia* (1974):

Individuals have rights, and there are things no person or group may do to them (without violating their rights). So strong and far-reaching are these rights they raise the question of what, if anything, the state and its officials may do. (p. 6)

Wilson (1978) then established that, although the premises of these two authors are put forward as beyond dispute, they are different in content and lead to radically different prescriptions.[16] He concludes that

philosophers, as anyone else, measure their personal emotional responses to various alternatives as though consulting a hidden oracle. That oracle resides in the deep emotional centers of the brain. . . . Human emotional responses and the more general ethical practices based on them have been programmed to a substantial degree by natural selection, over thousands of generations. (p. 6)

The real challenge then lies in the following: measuring the degree of rigor of the constraints caused by the genetic programming and decoding them, and determining in this framework the guidelines of humanity that must be listened to and those that must be rejected. Wilson concludes by asserting:

Consequences of genetic history cannot be chosen by legislature. For our own physical well being, if nothing else, ethical philosophy must not be left in the hands of the merely wise. Although human progress can be achieved by intuition and force of will, only hard-won empirical knowledge of our biological nature will allow us to make optimal choices among the competing criteria of progress. (1978, p. 7)

Along the same lines, Hirshleifer (1980) and Rodgers (1982) have argued that certain laws are more likely than others to promote group survival and that sociobiological explanations agree reasonably well with many legal principles that are actually observed.

A less ambitious approach is that of the economic theories of legal evolution. They consider that law is subject to certain selective processes likely to favor the emergence and the predominance of rules consistent with efficiency requirements (Posner 1977). Let me stress, however, that these approaches are not based on the idea that law has a genetic origin but on the hypothesis that in certain judicial fields, essentially the domain of rules relating to classic civil law and to common law developed by judges, there exist selection mechanisms operating in a way that is analogous to genetic selection. The predominance of "efficient" rules of law results not from the visible hand of the judge but from an invisible hand that intervenes by means of the decisions of the different parties to litigate rather than settling amicably. The basic theme is that an inefficient decision (rule), that is, a decision not in favor of the party capable of assigning the corresponding resource to the most efficient use, would be questioned more frequently, because losers have more to gain from a reversal of the decision than winners from its reaffirmation. More specifically, these models establish that judicial rules evolve in favor of those who have more at stake. A well-known theme, based on Coase's theorem, is that a party expecting an unfavorable decision and anxious to avoid a judgment will be willing to pay a total amount that is not higher than the expected loss from the judgment. Conversely, if a party expects to win, it would be dissuaded from going to court by a compensation marginally higher than its expected gain. It is therefore clear that the party with much at stake can always offer compensation to avoid a trial that it thinks it will lose, whereas the party with the least at stake cannot offer a sufficiently high amount to induce the other party to renounce a trial that it thinks it will win. Therefore the party with the highest stake will ensure that the only disputes taken to court are those that it expects to win. Because new judgments tend to modify the law in favor of winning parties, there is an evolution favoring those with the highest stakes.[17] These models have severe limitations, even in an analogical framework. First, the selection process rests on unusual hypotheses, and various authors have stressed their artificial character (Cooter and Kornhauser 1980). Second, the concept of efficiency here is ambiguous and refers to the maximization of wealth.[18] For an evolution of judicial rules in favor of those with higher stakes to be an evolution toward Pareto efficiency, it is first necessary that the size of stakes and prevention costs be positively correlated. Indeed, because in theory the cost of prevention ought to be less with an efficient rule, evolution in favor of the parties with higher stakes would go toward efficiency if those parties avoid the costs of prevention with more difficulty than the parties with lower stakes. However, it is not at all clear whether parties with lower stakes are better able than others to prevent or reduce the cost of the accidents, conflicts, and human interactions (Hollander and Mackaay 1982).

With regard to differences in the importance of stakes, it must also be noted that the gain of parties linked with the attribution of a right is influenced by the possible holding of monopoly power, which may be exploited in the exercise of this right. The party holding such power (or a power superior to the other party) will then be prepared to spend more to obtain this right even though social welfare could be better served by a different attribution. The lawsuit itself depends on the capacity to mobilize one's forces and on the income constraint affecting the parties in question. Pressures in favor of efficiency are also pressures favoring the rich at the expense of the poor, because they rest on the will and the ability to pay (Arrow, in Zerbe 1982, p. 194): Given that transaction costs and costs of changing a rule are positive, the poor are not necessarily able to pay the amount required to change a rule that is socially inefficient. The point is reinforced if one considers the rich to be generally less risk averse than the poor. By taking the case to a tribunal, the rich could impose a higher risk on the poor and obtain a more favorable decision. This would lead to a systematic redistributive effect that would be prejudicial to the poor. Finally, one could also raise the point of the waste of resources entailed by an increased number of actions and lawsuits aimed at sustaining strategic behavior.

So far as history is concerned, sociobiology is opposed to the theories put forward over the past few years along the lines of Popper. In his famous book, *The Poverty of Histori-*

cism (1957), Popper attacks the theories of J. S. Mill, A. Comte,[19] G. Vico,[20] and A. Toynbee.[21] Popper states that mankind's history is irreversible, nonlinear, and discontinuous and that it consists of acceleration and deceleration. The course of this history is profoundly influenced by the growth of human knowledge itself. Now, it is not possible to predict today one's future discoveries and their implications through modifications in initial conditions. Therefore one cannot extrapolate the tendency or the direction of an evolutionary movement because there is no scientific law behind it.

A trend (we may take population growth as an example) which has persisted for hundreds or even thousands of years may change within a decade, or even more rapidly than that (Popper 1957, p. 115)

And so far as natural evolution based on certain propensities of human nature toward a better world is concerned, this has no serious basis.[22] The conditions for such progress are numerous, including certain social and political institutions, but most of these conditions cannot be qualified as necessary (without them, progress is not impossible), and together they are not sufficient (even the best of institutions cannot guarantee progress that rests partly on chance). Hence observation of mankind's history in no way discloses the existence of mechanisms ensuring convergence toward certain types of behavior, organization, or regimes that can be qualified as better.[23]

According to the Wilsonian doctrine, history must be interpreted in the framework of genetic reproduction and propagation. This biohistory would be the only one that can shed light on laws of history. Wilson (1978) wrote:

One of the great dreams of social theories—Vico, Marx, Spencer, Teggart and Toynbee among the most innovative—has been to devise laws of history that can foretell something of the future of mankind. These schemes came to little because their understanding of human nature had no scientific basis. . . . The invisible hand remained invisible. . . . Now, there is reason to entertain the view that the culture of each society travels along one or the other of a set of evolutionary trajectories whose full array is constrained by the genetic rules of human nature. . . . As social sciences mature into predictive disciplines, the permissible trajectories will not only diminish in number, but our descendants will be able to sight farther along them. (p. 215)

6.3 Selection and Power in Industrial Society

In the previous section I tried to suggest that the methodological approach, based on the idea that competitive processes ensure the survival of the fittest, easily leads to (and has led to, in many recent, widely diffused writings) global vision, which claims to have the scientific bases for solving the big ethical and political problems of our society. Because this book is not intended to analyze such pretensions,[24] this section is confined to discussing the ambiguities and abusive simplifications affecting these studies, briefly suggesting the weakness of the biological basis that underlies sociobiology, and, finally, elaborating the characteristics of an approach in which the strategic dimension of socioeconomic behavior is recognized.

Biological analogies and parallels between biology and economics are a priori likely to encourage a better understanding of our societies. First, they encourage a vision according to which economic agents, firms, nations, and various forms of social organization are in a continuous process of change. Compared with an approach that tends to favor excessively the analysis of equilibrium conditions and stationary states, they seek to elucidate the process itself and the rich variety of mechanisms of change, such as mutation, selection, learning, or imitation.

Second, a biological perspective should facilitate the

liaison between the rational *homo economicus,* master of its choices on the one hand, and the role of biological heritage in the behavior of mankind on the other. The overlap between mankind and nature is better recognized here than in the usual economic approaches. Accounting for this mutual relationship could lead to a better understanding of our ecological insertion and the avoidance of anthropocentric illusions.[25]

On the other hand, the conceptions of society conveyed by the sociobiological approach are by no means acceptable. As we saw in section 6.2, selective mechanisms are described as adaptive processes that are more or less continuous and that ensure the emergence of an ideal type; these mechanisms are for their part interpreted as a prop for fundamental determinism.

Without pretending to tackle the debate in depth, I must first emphasize that the biological basis of this outlook has over the last few years proved to be much more fragile than one would have thought, whether it concerns the object of the selective process, the rhythm of evolution, or the selective character of this evolution. Thus, rather than a tendency toward a holotype within a species,[26] we observe the persistence of a significant *genetic polymorphism* corresponding to wide variability in morphological, physical, and psychological features that characterize individuals belonging to the same species. This polymorphism complies with the idea that the more a population is genetically polymorphous, the wider its horizon and the higher its chances of survival (see Ruffie (1982), p. 111). Contrary to the traditional viewpoint, the selective process is therefore not a standardizer, and it becomes difficult to define the best or the fittest.

What is good for a population, from the genetic point of view, is to be diverse. But being diverse means that characteristics must vary from one individual to another. One is then forbidden to make a judgement on each individual. (Jacquard 1979, p. 127)

Indeed current studies are exploring new approaches in which the target of natural selection is no longer the gene or even the individual but the population. In the same way, compared to "gradualist" pictures of evolution, in which change is slow and progressive, a "revolutionary" perspective has developed, in which change is rapid and proceeds by leaps: Periods of stability are interrupted by rapid speciations. As noted in chapter 2, the application of mathematical results on nonlinear systems to the field of biology in general suggests that, as opposed to the image of an ecological world tending toward a stationary stable state, the presence of nonlinear interactions in a population implies the possibility of cycles, of amplification of small errors, and of transition toward turbulence in biological and ecological systems.[27] Finally, various recent models explore the approach according to which the various genes are neutral, that is, not subject to selection, and in which changes in their frequency within a finite population are due to stochastic processes.[28]

When biological concepts are extrapolated to the social and economic domains, ambiguities, changes of meaning, and abusive extrapolations reach a stage at which the very purpose of the analogies is questioned. A first aspect, already mentioned in section 6.2, is the criterion of success and efficiency. If the usual criterion in biological evolution is that of relative success in reproduction or multiplication of the species, this is not the case in economics, even if it can be asserted that the underlying utility functions (or preference) are partially the outcome of genetic selection.[29] On the contrary, the question is to determine on the basis of the set of individual preferences if their lot can be improved with respect to these preferences. Unless one assumes that the system of preferences is merely the search for genetic continuity, it is not clear what contribution sociobiology makes in this matter. Recognition of the existence of an evolutionary process does not imply a tendency toward a natural social order and does not justify claiming that norms of human behavior in such an order have been established.

A second aspect is central to the perspective of this book: the role of behavior deliberately chosen to control and transform the environment.

In the first stage characteristics of human knowledge and its transmission deserve some discussion. As shown by Popper (1972), this knowledge is not simply an instrument in the fight for survival; it is driven by an internal logic continually urging it to develop further. "From the amoeba to Einstein is just one step," he writes (p. 246). But he adds:

> There is a great difference in their attitudes towards error. Einstein, unlike the amoeba, consciously tried his best, whenever a new solution occurred to him to fault it and detect an error in it: he approached his own solutions critically. (p. 246)

This method made it possible for Einstein "to reject, quickly, hundreds of hypotheses as inadequate before examining one or another hypothesis more carefully, if it appeared to be able to stand up to more serious criticism" (Popper 1972, p. 246). While the knowledge of the amoeba is subjective, based on disposition and expectations, the knowledge of Einstein is objective, reflecting the argumentative function of speech and allowing the conscious and critical attitude characteristic of the scientific method. In his "fundamental theorem" Popper draws the following conclusion:[30]

> All acquired knowledge, all learning, consists of the modification (possibly the rejection) of some form of knowledge, or disposition, which was there previously and in the last instance of inborn dispositions. (p. 71)

Transmission of this knowledge is then carried out through specific mechanisms. It is known that Lamarck was mistaken in assuming in his theory of change that changes brought about in the individual by the action of the environment are hereditary. For Lamarck, for instance, progressive development of the palmate of sea mammals and birds is due to the fact that these animals try to spread their fingers while swimming.[31] But, although in theory there is no heredity in somatic variations (which would imply the modification of the genotype and not simply the phenotype), it is clear that acquired cultural, scientific, social, indeed ethical knowledge is transmitted "hereditarily" and rapidly from one individual to another through various forms of apprenticeship and education that widen the space of strategies in an extraordinary fashion. The mechanism of this transmission and their more or less selective character are a priori unrelated to genetic mechanisms and are not well known. The least one knows is that the nature of those who control the education system and the means of communication, their objectives, and their strategies will influence the selected message and the dominant sociocultural model. Culture is then perceived as being more often deliberately chosen rather than biologically predetermined.

While selection enables living species to adapt themselves to a natural environment or to better resist changes in it, where man is concerned this environment ceases to be truly natural: it draws its distinctive features from technical, economic, social and mental conditions that create, through the working of culture, a particular environment for each human group.[32] (Lévi-Strauss 1983, p. 41)

As for genetic manipulations, we can even say that adopted forms of culture determine the rhythm and orientation of the biological evolution of mankind much more than these forms are determined by biological evolution.

The world of economics responds particularly well to this conception. As shown in previous chapters, social and

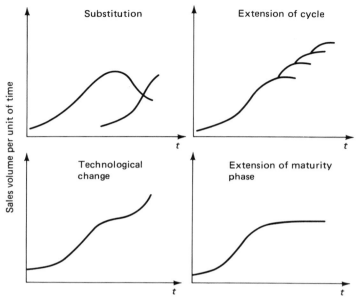

Figure 6.1
Industrial strategies modifying a product's life cycle.

economic evolution is characterized by deliberate modifications of the existing order. The entrepreneur, as described by Schumpeter, is not satisfied with detecting in-
variabilities in its environment and adjusting itself to these
in the best possible way: The entrepreneur introduces new
products and new systems of production and organization, thus rupturing repetitive processes and provoking
mutations. For example, determinism of the product's life
cycle, as evoked in section 2.3, is particularly ruptured
through various private or public industrial strategies (see
figure 6.1.) Simple mechanical laws of evolution lose their
relevance as a result of such strategies as introduction of a
new generation of products (substitution), implementation
of minor innovations that modify the characteristics of the

initial product (extension of the cycle), boosting demand through new technologies that allow lowering of costs and prices (technological change), and stabilization of demand over time thanks particularly to growing internationalization (extension of maturity phase). For the purpose of illustration, it is no doubt difficult to imagine a substitute for the automobile sector (except maybe the electric car); on the other hand, the extension of the cycle is realized thanks to electronics, and a crucial technological change is achieved through robotization (see van Duijn (1983)).

Therefore, because of various scientific, industrial, and commercial revolutions, abrupt changes do indeed occur and qualitative leaps are taken, thus modifying irreversibly production and consumption modes. The same holds true for the numerous transformations of economic and political regimes provoked by groups of privileged actors. The phenomenon has a long history. In the introduction to his monumental work, *Material Civilization, the Economy, and Capitalism,* the famous French historian Braudel (1979) emphasized that today's multinational capitalism is indeed related to the great East Indian Companies and the monopolies of rights and deeds that existed in the old days.

Isn't it right to maintain that the firms of the Fuggers and the Welsers were transnational . . . since they were interested in the whole of Europe and had representatives both in India and in Spanish America? Didn't the business of Jacques Coeur, in the last century, have similar dimensions, from the Netherlands to Levant? . . . Now such actors have been able to change greatly whole sectors of the European, indeed of the world economy. They bias exchange to their benefit, upsetting the established order. . . . They create anomalies and turbulences. (vol. 1, p. 9)

As Lévi-Strauss (1983) noted, recognition of the existence of strategic choices that deliberately transform the existing environment is for sociobiology the origin of a serious contradiction. Using a well-known criticism of the deterministic thesis, Lévi-Strauss wrote:

On the one hand, it is asserted that all forms of activity of the spirit are determined by inclusive adaptation; on the other, that we can modify the destiny of our species by consciously choosing from among instinctive orientations that our biological past has bequeathed to us. But only one of two things: either these choices are themselves dictated by requirements of the all-powerful inclusive adaptation, and we are still obeying it when we think we are choosing; or the possibility of choice is real, and it can no longer be said that human destiny is governed solely by genetic heritage. (p. 57).

In a framework in which socioeconomic order is indeed the partial outcome of chosen strategies, it is therefore important to bring to light asymmetries in endowment, perception, and motivation that confer the power of choice at the time of bifurcations, which either happen spontaneously or are provoked deliberately. If productive and organizational structures are no longer the outcome of some sort of natural necessity and if relations of power, in a context of scarcity, become a central issue, then one is equally forced to study within our decentralized economies instruments likely to ensure a better compatibility between individual interest and public interest. This is particularly the role of competition and industrial policies. Moreover, legal aspects of the intervention of public authorities in economic life find their full meaning. Contrary to common practice, rules of law should be used less as a deterring constraint, acting as an obstacle of efficiency, and more as a decision variable likely to promote the functioning of the system. Alternative forms of institutions, judicial organizations, and regulations should be compared in order to choose those that are best capable of regulating the economic situation in question. Legal analysis and its logic are thus at one with economic analysis in the concern to develop a blueprint for society.

It seems to me that this blueprint for society should address two major concerns. At a time when research in biology emphasizes the positive role of genetic polymorphism of populations, ensuring diversification in aptitudes and variety in activities, such a project should first encourage economic pluralism and value differences among individuals and among organizations, whether it concerns types of activity and employment, form and size of enterprises, the pace of work, or modes of consumption. Similarly, law is able to avoid trivializing social expectations and to legitimize taking into account various forms of social relations and the respect of minorities. Rather than seeing in this diversity an obstacle to harmony among people, law should be grasped as a generator of exchange and an active element of all true communication. Second, it is important to limit accumulation processes, consolidation, and perpetuation of positions of domination and to encourage regular redistribution of cards and mobility of positions. It is not hierarchy based on competence, responsibility, initiative, and creativity that is being questioned; it is the upholding of inequalities resting on carefully looked after privileges and on corporate rents of public or private origin.

In contrast to a uniform world in which competition rules in its purity and perfection, anonymous agents adapt themselves without the slightest strategy, and all individual initiative is devoted to homogenization and insignificance, our industrial universe is that of an irreducible plurality of preference and power. Grasping this reality in its diversity and movement is an important objective for both the scientist and the policymaker. From this viewpoint recent work on the new industrial organization is likely to clarify the stakes. Through the hypotheses that are chosen, the models proposed, the analogies used, and the forms of industrial policy considered we must be conscious of the emergence of fundamental choices capable of transforming the future of our societies.

Notes

1. From this viewpoint, Hillman's (1982) model is interesting. Starting from the hypothesis that public authorities maximize their political support rather than their social welfare function, Hillman concluded that "protective" interventions in a declining industry perpetuate the decline and that the authorities could just as easily accelerate the rate of decline as reduce it!

2. In the study by Encaoua in collaboration with Geroski and Miller (1983), it was shown that the degree of concentration and demand uncertainty have a negative effect on the degree of price flexibility, whereas international trade has a positive effect. See Dixon (1983) for the Australian case.

3. See, in particular, Chalmers (1982), who clarifies for MITI the progressive change from imperative procedures to processes of flexible concertedness.

4. Among these, let me point out the insistence on the role of the firm as a place of social integration, the necessity of constantly improving professional qualification and of sustaining diversity in aptitudes linked with a high level of general education, and finally the priority given to management of human resources over management of finance capital.

5. This example is based on Krugman (1984). For various works on this subject, see especially Auquier and Caves (1979), Itoh and Ono (1982), Spencer and Brander (1983), and Dixit (1984). For a brief survey, see Jacquemin (1982).

6. These developments are taken from Geroski and Jacquemin (1985).

7. The ESPRIT program is precisely intended to promote intracommunity cooperative research in five basic areas: microelectronics, software, information processing, office systems, and computer manufacturing technologies.

8. For the European situation, see Pinder (1981), Curzon-Price (1981), and Jacquemin (1984). For the American case, see Wachter and Wachter (1983), Tyson and Zysman (1983), and Adams and Klein (1983).

9. Recall that a gene is the basic unit of heredity. It is composed of the giant molecule DNA (deoxyribonucleic acid), which affects

the development of all characteristics at the most elementary biochemical level.

10. The genetic basis of this approach is that the degree of altruism depends on the number of common genes. The following calculation shows a simplified case. Assume that a parent has a gene that is relatively rare in the genetic pool, implying that each of the parent's cells contains a copy of this gene. Given that half of the sexual cells contain the rare gene and that any child can develop from one of these cells, there exists a 50% chance that a child will inherit the rare gene. The index of relatedness, that is, the chance that two related people share a gene, is equal to ½ in the case of the relationship between a parent and its child.

More generally, to determine the relation index between A and B, we proceed as follows. The common ancestor must first be identified. The next step is to count the number of necessary steps to go up from A to this ancestor and then add on the number of steps to go down from the ancestor to B. The index is equal to ½ raised to a power equal to the total number of steps. If there is more than one common ancestor, the separate indexes calculated for each ancestor must then be added. Assume the relation between an uncle (A) and a nephew (B). There is only one common ancestor, and that is the father of A, who is the grandfather of B. There is one step from A to his father and two steps from this father to B. The index of relatedness is therefore

$$r = (\tfrac{1}{2})^s = (\tfrac{1}{2})^3 = \tfrac{1}{8}.$$

In the case of two brothers, there is one step from A to the father and one step from the father to B:

$$r = (\tfrac{1}{2})^2,$$

but there are two common ancestors, that is, the father and the mother. The index is therefore

$$r = (\tfrac{1}{2})^2 + (\tfrac{1}{2})^2 = \tfrac{1}{2}.$$

An illustration by Dawkins (1976) indicates what the expected behavior would be if it were analyzed using a hypothesis that assumes that genetic reproduction is being maximized. Assume an animal who discovers eight mushrooms. After taking into account their nutritional value as well as the slight risk that they might be poisonous, the animal estimates that each mushroom has a value of 6 units. The size of the mushrooms is such that the animal can eat only three, and this makes it wonder if it should send a call to its fellow animals to share the food. It knows that its call will reach three individuals: a sibling ($r = \frac{1}{2}$), a cousin ($r = \frac{1}{8}$), and a third with such a distant relationship that r can be assumed equal to zero. It is, moreover, assumed that the eight mushrooms will be equally divided among the four individuals. If the animal abstains from calling, its net "genetic" gain is $3 \times 6 = 18$ units. If it makes the calls, the gain will correspond to the following sum: The two mushrooms eaten by the animal bring the total to 12 units; because the animal shares genes with its sibling and cousin, the units corresponding to mushrooms eaten by them must be added, weighted by the index of genetic relatedness. We have, therefore,

$$(1 \times 12) + (\tfrac{1}{2} \times 12) + (\tfrac{1}{8} \times 12) + (0 \times 12) = 19.5.$$

The conclusion is clear: It is better to make the call because this altruistic behavior favors the "egoistic" genes of the animal! The question is not whether the animal actually works out this kind of calculation but whether its observed behavior is a good approximation of this hypothesis. Friedman's methodology is not far off. In an interesting critique, Sahlins (1976) showed in particular that altruism is not manifested solely in favor of close parents and is equally exercised to the benefit of those who are "socially" close while being genetically far.

11. It is assumed that the gains, attributable to a phenotype (that is, the set of characters manifest in an individual), are linearly related to the genotype (G) (that is, the set of all hereditary genetic endowments fixed from fecundation) and to the environment or the investment in human capital (N):

$$y = aG + bN,$$

where the coefficients a and b depend on units in which the unobservable variables G and N are measured. The variance of gains can be written

$$\sigma_y^2 = a^2\sigma_G^2 + b^2\sigma_N^2 + 2ab\sigma_{GN}.$$

From these equations and based on a set of hypotheses, tests are carried out on a sample of twins allowing the estimation of $a^2\sigma_G^2$ and $b^2\sigma_N^2$. The conclusion is that 45% of the variance of ln y can be attributed to genetic causes. See Goldberger (1978) for a methodological critique. Some authors claim to have shown, in a much more radical form, that differences in intelligence (measured by IQ) have a genetic origin and are therefore hereditary. For a critical examination, see Taylor (1980). See also Leroy (1983), who throws some light on the role of cultural and political factors in income inequality.

12. This is from an interview published in *Business Week*, October 4, 1978.

13. See the discussion between Hirshleifer and Arrow in Zerbe (1982), particularly pp. 86 and 113.

14. For a stimulating survey on the evolutionary tradition in jurisprudence, see Elliott (1985).

15. Although Picard doubted whether law always evolves toward progress and evokes the role of "deviations" and "retrogressions," he did not hesitate to assert the "scientific" superiority of certain races. "Only the Aryan," he wrote (1897, p. 242), "can essentially be educated, is indefinitely progressive, inexhaustibly inventive, instinctively colonising"!

16. The theories of these authors are particularly subtle and require a thorough analysis. Let me simply mention that for Rawls some social control would be permissible in order to ensure a step as close as possible toward an egalitarian distribution of rewards brought by society; whereas for Nozick the ideal society is one governed by a state reduced to its simplest possible expression, having only the power to protect the citizens against force and fraud but allowing an unequal distribution of rewards.

17. The characteristics of the selective process vary according to different authors. Consider the following two illustrations. Some (see, for example, Goodman (1978)) assume that the outcome of a dispute is simply determined by the expenditures of the parties in a lawsuit: The winner is the one who spends the most. Moreover, given that with an efficient legal rule one of the parties will gain more from the reversal of the rule than the other will lose from its reaffirmation, each party is assumed to invest in judicial expenditures in proportion to the expected gain (or loss) of the other. The result of this is that only efficient rules will be amenable to new suits, and this mechanism will continue until the only prevailing rules are the efficient ones. Other authors (Priest 1977) explain the process differently. Assume two jurisdictions that are identical except that one uses an efficient rule and the other uses an inefficient rule. For road accidents, for instance, there will be a

priori more accidents within the jurisdiction in which the inefficient rule is in force, a larger amount of resources at stake in the set of all disputes likely to lead to legal action, a higher probability of lawsuits, and finally a higher probability of revision of the rule as a result of successive judgments. We can therefore expect a tendency toward "survival" of efficient rules, irrespective of differences in relative expenditures of the parties involved. However, Polinsky (in Zerbe (1982), p. 171) makes the remark that, for road accidents, if the existing rule is inefficient in the sense that the imposed norm is too demanding compared to what ought to be required, there will be fewer accidents in this jurisdiction than in the one where the efficient rule is applied.

18. In his study of primitive societies, Posner (1980, p. 53) adopted the same criterion: "The efficient society is wealthier than the inefficient one, this is the meaning of efficiency, and a wealthier society is capable of maintaining a larger population."

19. Let us recall the "law" of three states, according to which humanity, during its history, passes from the theological state to the metaphysical state and from the metaphysical state to the positivist state. Darwin was influenced by some of Comte's ideas.

20. G. Vico, in his *Principes d'une science nouvelle relative a la nature commune des nations* (Principles of a New Science on the Common Nature of Nations), distinguishes in the cyclical history of each people the divine age, the heroic age, and the human age.

21. In his *Study of History*, Toynbee considered that history is repetitive and that the laws of the life cycle of civilizations may be studied in the same way as the life cycle of some animal species. He declared his aim to be the empirical study of the life cycle of twenty-one specimens of the biological space "civilization"!

22. On this subject, Popper (1957, p. 118) quotes Mill, who wrote in his work on logic: "The general tendency is, and will continue to be, saving occasional and temporary exceptions, one of improvement—a tendency towards a happier and better state. This is a theorem of the (social) science."

23. Many historians have today taken up and refined this perspective and abandoned the myth of "scientific history." Although traditional historical accounts obey the logic of the narrative (post hoc, ergo propter hoc) and order past events along

a temporal path assumed to reflect the march of progress, so-called modern history certainly has the ambition to be "global knowledge, ecumenical, and uniting the conditions for maximal intelligibility of social phenomena" (Furet 1982, p. 9) but does not consider itself a science capable of finding the law that governs the appearance of an event. On the contrary, modern history seeks to avoid the traps of systematic rationalization of past evolution and is increasingly attentive to small disturbances that have triggered major evolution or given birth to the improbable.

24. An analysis of cultural background and social implications of sociobiology as well as an epistemological deciphering of corresponding writings are presented in Thuillier (1981a, 1981b). See also Valadier (1980). In his work with Lumsden (Lumsden and Wilson 1983), Wilson partially reversed his position (see p. 60 onward) when he recognized that the criticisms according to which important questions of humanity—relating to the spirit, the soul, culture, and history—are not covered by the field of sociobiology as originally formulated are largely well founded. He then proposed the theory of the "genes-culture coevolution," in which "culture is engendered and shaped by biological dictates while simultaneously, biological characteristics are altered by genetic evolution which reacts to cultural innovations" (Lumsden and Wilson 1983, p. 34).

25. See Moscovici (1972) for stimulating reflections on this theme.

26. Genetic selection is based on the idea that each genotype (association of genes) has a selective value in terms of the capacity to survive in the environment and to procreate. The genes that entail selective advantage will from one generation to the next increase in frequency in such a way that for a given environment the population will tend toward the ideal type possessing the best genes.

27. For an introductory article, see May (1976). It is on this basis that I. Prigogine, the Belgian Nobel Prize winner in chemistry, is opposed to the conception of J. Monod. For Monod there is deterministic universality of evolutionary laws, and the only law of macroscopic evolution that is predictable and reproducible is evolution toward equilibrium and the disappearance of all global activity. Only rare favorable mutations resulting from chance can

delay this "death." On the other hand, in the eyes of Prigogine and Stengers:

The notion of universal law gives place to that of the exploration of peculiar initial stabilities and instabilities, and the predictable generality of evolution they determine, gives place to coexistence of zones of divergence and zones of stability, to the dialectic of uncontrollable fluctuations and deterministic laws of averages. (Prigogine and Stengers 1979, p. 193)

28. See in particular, works by Kimura (1980) and Ohno (1980). This question is related to the eternal debate on determinism. A polemic defense of universal determinism is given by Thom (1980), whose tone contrasts with the nuanced response of Prigogine (1980). Let me emphasize that, so far as sociobiologists are concerned, the leap from affirmation of the role of selective mechanisms to that of determinism is unjustified. This aspect is again evoked when dealing with the biological explanation of socioeconomic choices.

29. Let me note that the sociobiological outlook implies convergence of preferences toward a system of "fundamental" preferences, thus facilitating interpersonal comparisons of utility. On the other hand, acceptance of individual preferences as the exclusive criterion would be a rash judgment if these preferences were believed to be strategically manipulated to some extent.

30. As pointed out by Malherbe (1976, p. 146 onward), it is Popper's proposition about the finality of science, conceived as the search for truth, that opposes the conception that knowledge should be understood as an instrument in the fight for survival. Knowledge cannot simply be reduced to a means of adaptation to environment and is fundamentally a modification of innate biological dispositions.

31. Roger (1979) explains how Kammerer, a disciple of Lamarck, had carried out experiments to show that some toads changed themselves according to transformations in their environment and were able to transmit hereditarily the variations thus induced. Kammerer committed suicide when an English scientist discovered that his tests were faked.

32. Similarly, Prigogine and Stengers (1979) wrote: "One can say that innovation is indeed selected, but by an environment that it has helped create. The driving force of the evolutionary process is

not selective pressure, its logic is not purely and simply that of environment's demands" (p. 185). Teilhard de Chardin (1955), for whom not only evolution but also genesis is becoming, had already noted: "In the great game that has been started, we are the players as well the cards and the stake" (p. 255).

References

F. G. Adams and L. Klein (eds.). 1983. *Industrial Policies for Growth and Competitiveness.* Lexington, MA: Lexington Books.

A. Auquier and R. Caves. 1979. "Monopolistic export industries, trade taxes, and optimal competition policy." *Economic Journal* 89:559–581.

G. Becker. 1976. "Altruism, egoism, and genetic fitness: Economics and sociobiology." *Journal of Economic Literature* 14:817–826.

P. Beneton. 1977. "Les aléas de la poursuite de l'égalité" (The hazards of pursuing equality). *Analyses de la SEDEIS* 1:3–10.

F. Braudel. 1979. *Material Civilization, the Economy, and Capitalism.* Paris: Colin.

J. Chalmers. 1982. *MITI and the Japanese Miracle: The Growth of Industrial Policy.* Stanford: Stanford University Press.

R. Cooter and L. Kornhauser. 1980. "Can litigation improve the law without the help of judges?" *Journal of Legal Studies* 9:139–163.

A. Coughlan and M. Flaherty. 1983. "Measuring the international marketing productivity of US semiconductor companies," in *Production and Efficiency in Distribution*, D. Gautchi (ed.). Amsterdam: Elsevier, 80–94.

V. Curzon-Price. 1981. *Industrial Policies in the European Community.* London: Macmillan.

R. Dawkins. 1976. *The Selfish Gene.* Oxford: Oxford University Press.

H. Demsetz. 1982. *Economic, Legal and Political Dimensions of Competition.* Amsterdam: North-Holland.

A. Dixit. 1984. "International trade policy for oligopolistic industries." *Economic Journal* 94:1–16.

A. Dixit and A. Kyle. 1985. "The use of protection and subsidies for entry promotion and deterrence." *American Economic Review* 75:139–152.

R. Dixon. 1983. "Industry structure and the speed of price adjustment." *Journal of Industrial Economics* 32(1):25–37.

J. M. Domenach. 1981. *Enquête sur les idées contemporaines* (Survey of contemporary ideas). Paris: Seuil.

E. Elliott. 1985. "The evolutionary tradition in jurisprudence." *Columbia Law Review* 38:40–94.

D. Encaoua, with P. Geroski and R. Miller. 1983. *Flexibilité cyclique des prix et inflation* (Cyclical flexibility of prices and inflation). Paris: OECD.

H. Ergaz. 1984. "Why do some countries innovate more than others?" CEPS Working paper, May.

F. Furet. 1982. *L'atelier de l'histoire* (The workshop of history). Paris: Flammarion.

P. Geroski and A. Jacquemin. 1985. "Industrial changes, barriers to mobility, and European industrial policy." *Economic Policy* 1:170–201.

M. Ghiselin. 1974. *The Economy of Nature and the Evolution of Sex.* Berkeley: University of California Press.

M. Ghiselin. 1978. "The economy of the body." *American Economic Review* 68(2):233–237.

A. Goldberger. 1978. "The genetic determination of income: A comment." *American Economic Review* 68(5):960–969.

J. Goodman. 1978. "An economic theory of the evolution of the common law." *Journal of Legal Studies* 7:393–406.

A. Hillman. 1982. "Declining industries and political support for protectionist motives." *American Economic Review* 72(5):1180–1187.

O. Hirschman. 1971. *Exit, Voice and Loyalty.* Cambridge: Harvard University Press.

J. Hirshleifer. 1978. "Competition, cooperation, and conflict in economics and biology." *American Economic Review* 68(2):238–243.

J. Hirshleifer. 1980. "Privacy: Its origin, function, and future."
Journal of Legal Studies 9:649–665.

A. Hollander and E. MacKaay. 1982. "Are judges economists at
heart?" in *Artificial Intelligence and Legal Information Systems,* C.
Ciampi (ed.). Amsterdam: North-Holland, 2–29.

M. Itoh and Y. Ono. 1982. "Tariffs, quotas and market structure."
Quarterly Journal of Economics 97(2):295–305.

F. Jacobs. 1970. *La logique du vivant* (The logic of the living). Paris:
Gallimard.

A. Jacquard. 1979. "Darwinisme et génétique des populations"
(Darwinism and population genetics), in *Le darwinisme aujourd'hui*
(Darwinism today). Paris: Seuil.

A. Jacquemin. 1982. "Imperfect market structure and international trade: Some recent research." *Kyklos* 35:75–93.

A. Jacquemin (ed.). 1984. *European Industry: Public Policy and Corporate Strategy.* Oxford: Oxford University Press.

M. Kierzkowski (ed.). 1983. *Monopolistic Competition and International Trade.* Oxford: Oxford University Press.

M. Kimura. 1980. "La théorie neutraliste de l'évolution
moléculaire" (The neutral theory of molecular evolution). *Pour la
Science* 27:6–18.

P. Krugman. 1984. "The US response to foreign industrial target-
ing," in *Brookings Papers on Economic Activity,* W. Brainard and G.
Perry (eds.). Washington, D.C.: Brookings Institution, 77–121.

R. Leroy. 1983. *Un scénario égalitaire* (An egalitarian scenario).
Louvain-la-Neuve: Ciaco.

C. Lévi-Strauss. 1971. "Race et culture" (Race and culture). *Revue
internationale des Sciences Sociales,* UNESCO. Reprinted in Lévi-
Strauss (1983).

C. Lévi-Strauss. 1983. *Le regard éloigné* (The distant look). Paris:
Plon.

C. Lumsden and E. Wilson. 1983. *Promethean Fire.* Cambridge:
Harvard University Press.

J. F. Malherbe. 1976. *La philosophie de Karl Popper et le positivisme
logique* (The philosophy of Karl Popper and logical positivism).
Paris: PUF.

R. May. 1976. "Simple mathematical models with very complicated dynamics." *Nature* 261:459–467.

J. Monod. 1970. *Le hasard et la nécessité* (Chance and necessity). Paris: Seuil.

S. Moscovici. 1972. *La société contre nature* (Society versus nature). Paris: Union Générale d'Editions.

R. Nozick. 1974. *Anarchy, State and Utopia.* Oxford: Blackwell.

OECD. 1972. *The Industrial Policy in Japan.* Paris: OECD.

OECD. 1985. *The Semi-conductor Industry.* Paris: OECD.

S. Ohno. 1980. "L'evolution des genes" (The evolution of genes). *La Recherche* 11:24–36.

E. Picard. 1897. *Le droit pur* (Pure law). Bruxelles: Larcier.

J. Pinder (ed.). 1981. *National Industrial Strategies and the World Economy.* Totowa, NJ: Allanheld.

K. Popper. 1957. *The Poverty of Historicism.* New York: Harper & Row.

K. Popper. 1972. *Objective Knowledge: An Evolutionary Approach.* Oxford: Oxford University Press.

R. Posner. 1977. *Economic Analysis of Law,* second edition. Boston: Little, Brown.

R. Posner. 1980. "A theory of primitive society with special reference to primitive law." *Journal of Law and Economics* 23(1):1–53.

G. Priest. 1977. "The common law process and the selection of efficient rules." *Journal of Legal Studies* 6:65–83.

I. Prigogine. 1980. "Loi, histoire . . . et désertion" (Law, history and desertion). *Le Débat* 3:122–130.

I. Prigogine and I. Stengers. 1979. *La nouvelle alliance* (The new alliance). Paris: Gallimard.

J. Rawls. 1971. *A Theory of Justice.* Cambridge: Harvard University Press.

W. Rodgers. 1982. "Bringing people back: Toward a comprehensive theory of taking in natural resources law." *Ecology Law Quarterly* 10:205–230.

J. Roger. 1979. "Le transformisme de Lamarck" (The transformism of Lamarck), in *Le darwinisme aujourd'hui* (Darwinism today). Paris: Seuil.

J. Ruffie. 1982. *Traité du vivant* (Treatise of the living). Paris: Fayard.

M. Sahlins. 1976. *The Use and Abuse of Biology: An Anthropological Critique of Sociobiology*. Ann Arbor: University of Michigan Press.

A. Sen. 1980. "Description as choice." *Oxford Economic Papers*, November, 353–369.

A. Simon. 1973. "Les marques de la violence" (Signs of violence). *Esprit* 3:2–26.

B. Spencer and J. Brander. 1983. "International R & D and industrial strategy." *Review of Economic Studies* 50:707–722.

P. Taubman. 1976. "The determinants of earnings: Genetics, family, and other environments; a study of white male twins." *American Economic Review* 66(5):858–850.

P. Taubman. 1978. "What we learn from estimating the genetic contribution to inequality of earnings: Reply." *American Economic Review* 68(5):970–976.

H. Taylor. 1980. *The I.Q. Game: A Methodological Inquiry into the Heredity-Environment Controversy*. New Brunswick, NJ: Rutgers University Press.

P. Teilhard de Chardin. 1955. *Le phénomène humain* (The human phenomenon). Paris: Seuil.

R. Thom. 1980. "Halte au hasard, silence au bruit" (Stopping fate, silencing noise). *Le Débat* 3:119–132.

P. Thuillier. 1981a. *Les biologistes vont-ils prendre le pouvoir?* (Will the biologists take power?). Bruxelles: Editions Complexe.

P. Thullier. 1981b. *Darwin & Co* (Darwin and Company). Bruxelles: Editions Complexe.

J. Tilton. 1972. *The International Diffusion of Technology: The Case of Semiconductors*. Washington, D.C.: Brookings Institution.

M. Tyson and K. Zysman. 1983. *American Industry in International Competition: Government Policies and Corporate Strategies*. Ithaca: Cornell University Press.

P. Valadier. 1980. "Un nouveau totémisme: La sociobiologie" (The new totemism: Sociobiology). *Etudes*, August-September, 23–32.

J. J. van Duijn. 1983. *The Long Wave in Economic Life*. London: Allen & Unwin.

M. Wachter and S. Wachter (eds.). *Towards a New U.S. Industrial Policy?* Philadelphia: University of Pennsylvania Press.

E. Wilson. 1978. *On Human Nature*. Cambridge: Harvard University Press.

R. Zerbe (ed.). *Research in Law and Economics: Evolutionary Models in Economics and Law*. London: AIJAI Press.

Index

Page numbers in italics indicate tables or figures.